P9-CML-678

Inside Reading

THE ACADEMIC WORD LIST IN CONTEXT

By Lawrence J. Zwier

Series Director: Cheryl Boyd Zimmerman

2

OXFORD

UNIVERSITY PRESS

OXFORD
UNIVERSITY PRESS

198 Madison Avenue
New York, NY 10016 USA

Great Clarendon Street, Oxford OX2 6DP UK

Oxford University Press is a department of the University of Oxford.
It furthers the University's objective of excellence in research, scholarship,
and education by publishing worldwide in

Oxford New York

Auckland Cape Town Dar es Salaam Hong Kong Karachi
Kuala Lumpur Madrid Melbourne Mexico City Nairobi
New Delhi Shanghai Taipei Toronto

With offices in

Argentina Austria Brazil Chile Czech Republic France Greece
Guatemala Hungary Italy Japan Poland Portugal Singapore
South Korea Switzerland Thailand Turkey Ukraine Vietnam

OXFORD and OXFORD ENGLISH are registered trademarks of
Oxford University Press.

© Oxford University Press 2009

Database right Oxford University Press (maker)

Library of Congress Cataloging-in-Publication Data
Burgmeier, Arline
    Inside reading 1: the academic word list in context / Arline Burgmeier.
    p. cm.
    ISBN 978-0-19-441612-2 (pbk. w/ cdrom)
    1. English language—Textbooks for foreign speakers. 2. Vocabulary. I. Title.
PE1128.B846 2007
    428.2'4—dc22   2007023406

No unauthorized photocopying.

All rights reserved. No part of this publication may be reproduced,
stored in a retrieval system, or transmitted, in any form or by any means,
without the prior permission in writing of Oxford University Press,
or as expressly permitted by law, or under terms agreed with the appropriate
copyright clearance organization. Enquiries concerning reproduction outside
the scope of the above should be sent to the ELT Rights Department, Oxford
University Press, at the address above.

You must not circulate this book in any other binding or cover
and you must impose this same condition on any acquirer.

Any websites referred to in this publication are in the public domain and
their addresses are provided by Oxford University Press for information only.
Oxford University Press disclaims any responsibility for the content.

Editorial Director: Sally Yagan
Senior Managing Editor: Patricia O'Neill
Editor: Dena Daniel
Design Director: Robert Carangelo
Design Manager: Maj-Britt Hagsted
Production Artist: Julie Armstrong
Compositor: TSI Graphics Inc.
Cover design: Stacy Merlin
Production Manager: Shanta Persaud
Production Controller: Eve Wong

Student book pack ISBN: 978 0 19 441613 9

Student book ISBN: 978 0 19 441603 0

Printed in Hong Kong

10 9 8 7 6 5 4 3 2 1

ACKNOWLEDGMENTS

Cover art: Getty Images: William Shakespeare; IT Stock Free/Jupiter Images: Bee

The publisher would like to thank TSI Graphics for the illustrations used in this book.

*The publisher would like to thank the following for their permission to reproduce
photographs*: Peter McLaren/Beaut Photos: 3; Alessandro Gandolfi/Jupiter Images:
4; Shihi Fukada/AP Images: 8; Matt Blaze: 9; David Spindel/SuperStock: 16;
Time & Life Pictures/Getty Images: 17; Lars Klove: 23; image100/SuperStock: 30;
Ewing Galloway/Jupiter Images: 44; Mary Evans Picture Library/Alamy: 44; The
Print Collector/Alamy: 51; Wallace Kirkland/Time & Life Pictures/Getty Images:
80; Dennis O'Clair/Jupiter Images: 101; Carrie Osgood/AP Images: 121; Eye of
Science/Photo Researchers, Inc: 128

*The publisher would like to thank the following for their permission to reproduce
copyrighted material*: pp. **3–4**, "Opal Fever: Adventures in the Outback," by
Kathy Marks, *The Independent*, March 10, 2002. Excerpted and adapted with
permission. pp. **8–10**, "The Ugly Underneath," by Amanda Gefter, *Philadelphia
City Paper*, September 7–13, 2006. Reprinted and adapted with permission.
pp. **16–17**, Interview quote from Kai Ryssdal, interviewer, National Public
Radio, "Marketplace," August 7, 2006. pp. **23–24**, "The Brand Underground," by
Rob Walker, *The New York Times Magazine*, July 30, 2006. © 2006 by Rob Walker.
Reprinted and adapted with permission. pp. **72–73**, "How to eat smart," by
Randy Braun and Andreas Wiesenack, *Psychology Today*. p. **60**, Adapted from
National Geographic Xpeditions, "Climographs: Temperature, Precipitation,
and the Human Condition." pp. **79–80**, "They Starved So That Others Be
Better Fed: Remembering Ancel Keys and the Minnesota Experiment," by
Leah M. Kalm and Richard D. Semba, *The Journal of Nutrition*, American Society
for Nutrition. Reprinted and adapted with permission. pp. **86–87**, Adapted
from U.S. Geologic Survey, "Plate Tectonics." pp. **92–93**, "In the land of
death, scientists witness the birth of a new ocean" by Xan Rice, *The Guardian*,
November 2, 2006. © 2006 by Guardian News & Media Ltd. Reprinted and
adapted with permission. pp. **100–101**, "Judging Roommates by Their
Facebook Cover," © 2006 by *The Chronicle of Higher Education*. Reprinted and
adapted with permission. Original version available at http://chronicle.com.
pp. **106–107**, "Terror in Littleton: The Teen-age Culture," by Tamar Lewin, *The
New York Times*, May 2, 1999, Late Edition - Final, Section 1, Page 28, Column 1.
Excerpted and adapted with permission. pp. **120–121**, "Don't Believe What
You See in the Papers: The Untrustworthiness of News Photography," by Jim
Lewis. Reprinted and adapted with permission. pp. **134–135**, *Bitten: True Medical
Stories of Bites and Stings*, by Pamela Nagani, M.D. © 2004 by St. Martin's Press,
New York.

Acknowledgments

From the Series Director

Inside Reading represents collaboration as it should be. That is, the project resulted from a balance of expertise from a team at Oxford University Press (OUP) and a collection of skilled participants from several universities. The project would not have happened without considerable investment and talent from both sides.

This idea took root and developed with the collaboration and support of the OUP editorial team. I am particularly grateful to Pietro Alongi, whose vision for this series began with his recognition of the reciprocal relationship between reading and vocabulary. I am also grateful to Dena Daniel, the lead editor on the project, and Janet Aitchison for her involvement in the early stages of this venture.

OUP was joined by the contributions of participants from various academic settings. First, Averil Coxhead, Massey University, New Zealand, created the Academic Word List, a principled, research-based collection of academic words which has led both to much of the research which supports this project and to the materials themselves. Dr. Tom Klammer, Dean of Humanities and Social Sciences at California State University, Fullerton (CSUF), made my participation in this project possible, first by endorsing its value, then by providing the time I needed. Assistance and insight were provided by CSUF participants Patricia Balderas, Arline Burgmeier, and Margaret Plenert, as well as by many TESOL Masters students at CSUF.

Finally, thank you to the many reviewers who gave us feedback along the way: Nancy Baum, **University of Texas at Arlington**; Adele Camus, **George Mason University**; Carole Collins, **Northampton Community College**; Jennifer Farnell, **University of Connecticut**, ALP; Laurie Frazier, **University of Minnesota**; Debbie Gold, **California State University**, Long Beach, ALI; Janet Harclerode and Toni Randall, **Santa Monica Community College**; Marianne Hsu Santelli, **Middlesex County College**; Steve Jones, **Community College of Philadelphia**; Lucille King, **University of Connecticut**; Shalle Leeming, **Academy of Art University**, San Francisco; Gerry Luton, **University of Victoria**; David Mindock, **University of Denver**; William Morrill, **University of Washington**; and Peggy Alptekin. This is collaboration indeed!

From the Author

Big thanks go out to everyone at Oxford University Press for their help and advice: To Pietro Alongi for bringing me into the series and showing me the ropes. To Cheryl Boyd Zimmerman for her truly exceptional ideas about effective vocabulary exercises and for her spot-on editorial work. To Dena Daniel for bringing flexibility, a fine sense of humor, and superb organizational skills to the hard task of turning it all into a real book. And finally to Glenn Mathes II for introducing me to this great team.

Contents

Unit 1 Going Underground   1

Unit 2 The Business of Branding   15

Unit 3 Machines That Recognize Faces   29

Unit 4 How Could They Do That?   43

Unit 5 Weather Warnings   57

To the Teacher

There is a natural relationship between academic reading and word learning. *Inside Reading* is a four-level reading and vocabulary series designed to use this relationship to best advantage. Through principled instruction and practice with reading strategies and skills, students will increase their ability to comprehend reading material. Likewise, through a principled approach to the complex nature of vocabulary knowledge, learners will better understand how to make sense of the complex nature of academic word learning. *Inside Reading 2* is intended for students at the intermediate level.

Academic Reading and Vocabulary: A Reciprocal Relationship

In the beginning stages of language learning, when the learner is making simple connections between familiar oral words and written forms, vocabulary knowledge plays a crucial role. In later stages, such as those addressed by *Inside Reading*, word learning and reading are increasingly interdependent: rich word knowledge facilitates reading, and effective reading skills facilitate vocabulary comprehension and learning.[1]

The word knowledge that is needed by the reader in this reciprocal process is more than knowledge of definitions.[2] Truly knowing a word well enough to use it in reading (as well as in production) means knowing something about its grammar, word forms, collocations, register, associations, and a great deal about its meaning, including its connotations and multiple meanings.[3] Any of this information may be called upon to help the reader make the inferences needed to understand the word's meaning in a particular text. For example, a passage's meaning can be controlled completely by a connotation

She was *frugal*. (positive connotation)

She was *stingy*.   (negative connotation)

by grammatical form

He valued his *memory*.

He valued his *memories*.

or an alternate meaning

The *labor* was intense. (physical work vs. childbirth)

Inside Reading recognizes the complexity of knowing a word. Students are given frequent and varied practice with all aspects of word knowledge. Vocabulary activities are closely related in topic to the reading selections, providing multiple exposures to a word in actual use and opportunities to work with its meanings, grammatical features, word forms, collocations, register, and associations.

To join principled vocabulary instruction with academic reading instruction is both natural and effective. *Inside Reading* is designed to address the reciprocal relationship between reading and vocabulary and to use it to help students develop academic proficiency.

A Closer Look at Academic Reading

Students preparing for academic work benefit from instruction that includes attention to the language as well as attention to the process of reading. The Interactive Reading model indicates that reading is an active process in which readers draw upon *top-down processing* (bringing meaning to the text), as well as *bottom-up processing* (decoding words and other details of language).[4]

The *top-down* aspect of this construct suggests that reading is facilitated by interesting and relevant reading materials that activate a range of knowledge in a reader's mind, knowledge that is refined and extended during the act of reading.

The *bottom-up* aspect of this model suggests that the learner needs to pay attention to language proficiency, including vocabulary. An academic reading course must address the teaching of higher-level reading strategies without neglecting the need for language support.[5]

---

[1] Koda, 2005

[2] See the meta-analysis of L1 vocabulary studies by Stahl & Fairbanks, 1986.

[3] Nation, 1990

[4] Carrell, Devine, and Eskey, 1988

[5] Birch, 2002; Eskey, 1988

Inside Reading addresses both sides of the interactive model. High-interest academic readings and activities provide students with opportunities to draw upon life experience in their mastery of a wide variety of strategies and skills, including

- previewing
- scanning
- using context clues to clarify meaning
- finding the main idea
- summarizing
- making inferences.

Rich vocabulary instruction and practice that targets vocabulary from the Academic Word List (AWL) provide opportunities for students to improve their language proficiency and their ability to decode and process vocabulary.

A Closer Look at Academic Vocabulary

Academic vocabulary consists of those words which are used broadly in all academic domains, but are not necessarily frequent in other domains. They are words in the academic register that are needed by students who intend to pursue higher education. They are not the technical words used in one academic field or another (e.g., *genetics, fiduciary, proton*), but are found in all academic areas, often in a supportive role (*substitute, function, inhibit*).

The most principled and widely accepted list of academic words to date is The Academic Word List (AWL), compiled by Averil Coxhead in 2000. Its selection was based on a corpus of 3.5 million words of running text from academic materials across four academic disciplines: the humanities, business, law, and the physical and life sciences. The criteria for selection of the 570 word families on the AWL was that the words appear frequently and uniformly across a wide range of academic texts, and that they not appear among the first 2000 most common words of English, as identified by the General Service List.[6]

Across the four levels of *Inside Reading*, students are introduced to the 570 word families of the AWL

at a gradual pace of about 15 words per unit. Their usage is authentic, the readings in which they appear are high interest, and the words are practiced and recycled in a variety of activities, facilitating both reading comprehension and word learning.

There has been a great deal of research into the optimal classroom conditions for facilitating word learning. This research points to several key factors.

Noticing: Before new words can be learned, they must be noticed. Schmidt, in his well-known *noticing hypothesis*, states

> noticing is the necessary and sufficient condition for converting input into intake. Incidental learning, on the other hand, is clearly both possible and effective when the demands of a task focus attention on what is to be learned.[7]

Inside Reading facilitates noticing in two ways. Target words are printed in boldface type at their first occurrence to draw the students' attention to their context, usage, and word form. Students are then offered repeated opportunities to focus on them in activities and discussions. *Inside Reading* also devotes activities and tasks to particular target words. This is often accompanied by a presentation box giving information about the word, its family members, and its usage.

Teachers can further facilitate noticing by pre-teaching selected words through "rich instruction," meaning instruction that focuses on what it means to know a word, looks at the word in more than one setting, and involves learners in actively processing the word.[8] *Inside Reading* facilitates rich instruction by providing engaging activities that use and spotlight target words in both written and oral practice.

Repetition: Word learning is incremental. A learner is able to pick up new knowledge about a word with each encounter. Repetition also assists learner memory—multiple exposures at varying intervals dramatically enhance retention.

Repetition alone doesn't account for learning; the types and intervals of repetitions are also important.

---

6   West, 1953; Coxhead 2000
7   Schmidt, 1990, p. 129
8   Nation, 2001, p. 157

Research shows that words are best retained when the practice with a new word is brief but the word is repeated several times at increasing intervals.[9] *Inside Reading* provides multiple exposures to words at varying intervals and recycles vocabulary throughout the book to assist this process.

Learner involvement: Word-learning activities are not guaranteed to be effective simply by virtue of being interactive or communicative. Activities or tasks are most effective when learners are most *involved* in them. Optimal involvement is characterized by a learner's own perceived need for the unknown word, the desire to search for the information needed for the task, and the effort expended to compare the word to other words. It has been found that the greater the level of learner involvement, the better the retention.[10]

The activities in *Inside Reading* provide opportunities to be involved in the use of target words at two levels:

- "Word level," where words are practiced in isolation for the purpose of focusing on such aspects as meaning, derivation, grammatical features, and associations.
- "Sentence level," where learners respond to the readings by writing and paraphrasing sentences.

Because the activities are grounded in the two high-interest readings of each unit, they provide the teacher with frequent opportunities to optimize learner involvement.

Instruction and practice with varying types of word knowledge: To know a word means to know a great deal about the word.[11] The activities in this book include practice with all aspects of word knowledge: form (both oral and written), meaning, multiple meanings, collocations, grammatical features, derivatives, register, and associations.

Helping students become independent word learners: No single course or book can address all of the words a learner will need. Students should leave a class with new skills and strategies for word learning so that they can notice and effectively practice new words as they encounter them. *Inside Reading* includes several features to help guide students to becoming independent word learners. One is a self-assessment activity, which begins and ends each unit. Students evaluate their level of knowledge of each word, ranging from not knowing a word at all, to word recognition, and then to two levels of word use. This exercise demonstrates the incremental nature of word knowledge, and guides learners toward identifying what they know and what they need to know. Students can make better progress if they accurately identify the aspects of word knowledge they need for themselves. Another feature is the use of references and online resources: To further prepare students to be independent word learners, instruction and practice in dictionary use and online resources are provided throughout the book.

The *Inside Reading* Program

Inside Reading offers students and teachers helpful ancillaries:

Student CD-ROM: The CD-ROM in the back of every student book contains additional practice activities for students to work with on their own. The activities are self-correcting and allow students to redo an activity as many times as they wish.

Instructor's pack: The Instructor's pack contains the answer key for the book along with a test generator CD-ROM. The test generator contains one test per student book unit. Each test consists of a reading passage related to the topic of the unit, which features the target vocabulary. This is followed by reading comprehension and vocabulary questions. Teachers can use each unit's test in full or customize it in a variety of ways.

Inside Reading optimizes the reciprocal relationship between reading and vocabulary by drawing upon considerable research and many years of teaching experience. It provides the resources to help students read well and to use that knowledge to develop both a rich academic vocabulary and overall academic language proficiency.

---

[9] Research findings are inconclusive about the number of repetitions that are needed for retention. Estimates range from 6 to 20. See Nation, 2001, for a discussion of repetition and learning.

[10] Laufer & Hulstijn, 2001

[11] Nation, 1990; 2001

References

Carrel, P.L., Devine, J., & Eskey, D.E. (1988). *Interactive approaches to second language reading.* Cambridge: Cambridge University Press. (Or use "Holding in the bottom" by Eskey)

Coxhead, A. (2000). A new academic word list. *TESOL Quarterly, 34,* 213–238.

Eskey, D.E. (1988). Holding in the bottom. In P.L. Carrel, J. Devine, & D.E. Eskey, *Interactive approaches to second language reading,* pp. 93–100. Cambridge: Cambridge University Press.

Koda, K. (2005). *Insights into second language reading.* Cambridge: Cambridge University Press.

Laufer, B. (2005). Instructed second language vocabulary learning: The fault in the 'default hypothesis'. In A. Housen & M. Pierrard (Eds.), *Investigations in Instructed Second Language Acquisition,* pp. 286–303. New York: Mouton de Gruyter.

Laufer, B. (1992). Reading in a foreign language: How does L2 lexical knowledge interact with the reader's general academic ability? *Journal of Research in Reading, 15*(2), 95–103.

Nation, I.S.P. (1990). *Teaching and learning vocabulary.* New York: Newbury House.

Nation, I.S.P. (2001). *Learning vocabulary in another language.* Cambridge: Cambridge University Press.

Schmidt, R. (1990). The role of consciousness in second language learning. *Applied Linguistics, 11,* 129–158.

Schmitt, N. (2000). *Vocabulary in language teaching.* Cambridge: Cambridge University Press.

Schmitt, N. & Zimmerman, C.B. (2002). Derivative word forms: What do learners know? *TESOL Quarterly, 36*(2), 145–171.

Stahl, S.A. & Fairbanks, M.M. (1986). The effects of vocabulary instruction: A model-based meta-analysis. *Review of Educational Research, 56*(1), 72–110.

Welcome to *Inside Reading*

Inside Reading is a four-level series that develops students' abilities to interact with and access academic reading and vocabulary, preparing them for success in the academic classroom.

There are ten units in *Inside Reading*. Each unit features two readings on a high-interest topic from an academic content area, one or more reading skills and strategies, and work with a set of target word families from the **Academic Word List**.

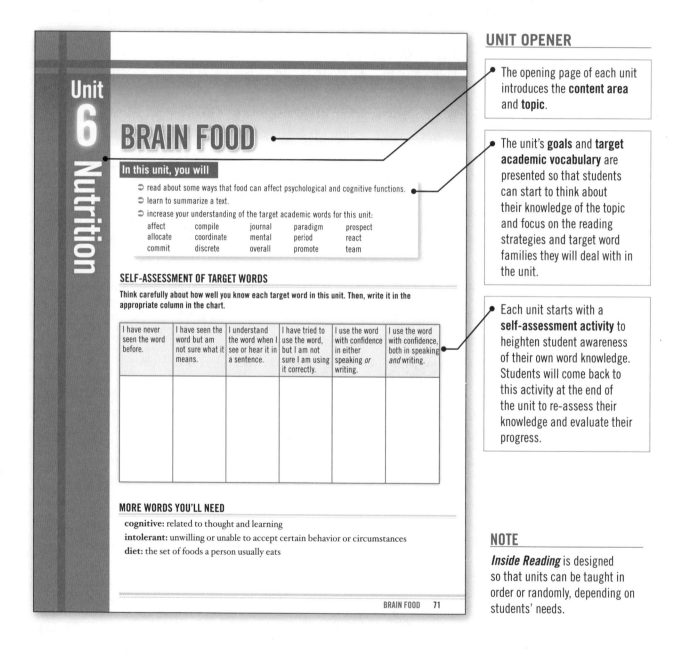

UNIT OPENER

The opening page of each unit introduces the **content area** and **topic**.

The unit's **goals** and **target academic vocabulary** are presented so that students can start to think about their knowledge of the topic and focus on the reading strategies and target word families they will deal with in the unit.

Each unit starts with a **self-assessment activity** to heighten student awareness of their own word knowledge. Students will come back to this activity at the end of the unit to re-assess their knowledge and evaluate their progress.

NOTE

Inside Reading is designed so that units can be taught in order or randomly, depending on students' needs.

READING 1

BEFORE YOU READ

Read these questions. Discuss your answers in a small group.

1. Name three or four foods you often eat even though you know they're not good for you. Why are they unhealthful? Why do you eat them anyway?

2. Name three or four foods you eat that are healthful. Why are they healthful? Do you like the way they taste?

3. Have you ever felt a significant improvement in your mood or in your concentration after a meal or snack? What do you think caused this effect?

READ

This excerpt from a nutrition manual explains the psychological benefits of eating certain fats.

Fat for Brains

As the old saying goes, you are what you eat. The foods you eat obviously **affect** your body's performance. They may also influence how your brain handles its tasks. If it handles them
5 well, you think more clearly and you are more emotionally stable. The right foods can help you concentrate, keep you motivated, sharpen your memory, speed your **reaction** time, defuse stress, and perhaps even prevent brain aging.

10 **Good and bad fat**

Most people associate the term *fat* with poor health. We are encouraged to eat fat-free foods and to drain fat away from fried foods. To understand its psychological benefits, however,
15 we have to change the **paradigm** for how we think about fat.

Foods that are high in saturated fats include meat, butter, and other animal products.
30 In general, saturated fats are solid at room temperature. Foods high in unsaturated fats include vegetable oils, nuts, and avocados. Unsaturated fats, if separated out, are usually liquid at room temperature.

Foods high in saturated fats

- Before each of the two readings in a unit, students discuss questions to **activate knowledge of the specific topic** dealt with in the reading.

- Readings represent **a variety of genres**: newspapers, magazines, websites, press releases, encyclopedias, and books.

- Target vocabulary is bold at its first occurrence to aid recognition. **Vocabulary is recycled** and practiced throughout the unit. Target words are also recycled in subsequent units.

READING COMPREHENSION

Reading comprehension questions follow each text to check students' understanding and recycle target vocabulary.

READING COMPREHENSION

Mark each sentence as *T* (true) or *F* (false) according to the information in Reading 1. Use the dictionary to help you understand new words.

.... 1. Foods affect a person's moods and motivation.

.... 2. Ideally, more people should commit to no-fat diets.

.... 3. At room temperature, you could pour unsaturated fat out of a bottle.

.... 4. It is not healthful to eat a very large amount of unsaturated fat.

.... 5. Omega-3 fatty acids promote intellectual development.

.... 6. Breast milk is a better source of DHA than infant formulas.

.... 7. Research journals reported that people with a lot of omega-3 fats in their systems were very depressed.

READING STRATEGIES

Strategy presentation and **practice** accompanies each reading.

READING STRATEGY: Making Inferences

When you make an inference, you use clues in a reading to understand something the author has not directly stated. The reading implies it, and you infer it. An inference is a conclusion that you draw from the information presented in the reading.

Read the paragraph indicated again. Then, select the one or two statements that can be most strongly inferred from each paragraph. Compare selections with a partner and explain your choices.

1. Paragraph 1:
   a. There are more small tectonic plates than large ones.
   b. The top layer of the mantle is liquid.
   c. The continents were formed from material in the mantle.
2. Paragraph 2:
   a. Catastrophists believed the Earth should not change.
   b. Catastrophists believed religion should not interfere with science.
   c. Catastrophists believed forces we now witness were not enough to shape the Earth.

VOCABULARY ACTIVITIES

The vocabulary work following each reading **starts at word level**. Step I activities are mostly receptive and focus on meanings and word family members.

STEP I VOCABULARY ACTIVITIES: Word Level

A. Read these excerpts from an article on tectonic plates. For each excerpt, cross out the one word or phrase in parentheses with a different meaning from the other three choices. Compare answers with a partner.

1. *Geodesy* is the study of the size and shape of the Earth. Over thousands of years, the tools of the field have (*fluctuated / developed / evolved / progressed*) so that now we can use geodetic measurements to track the movement of tectonic plates.
2. Because plate motions happen all over the globe at the same time, only satellite-based methods can give a truly (*all-inclusive / comprehensive / accurate / thorough*) view of them.
3. In the late 1970s, these space-based techniques completely (*improved / changed / altered / transformed*) the field of geodesy.
4. Of the space-based techniques, the Global Positioning System (GPS) has provided the most (*aid / assistance / truth / help*) to scientists studying the movements of the Earth's crust.
5. By repeatedly measuring distances between specific points, geologists can determine if there has been significant (*displacement / restraint / movement / repositioning*) among the plates.

Vocabulary work then **progresses to the sentence level**. Step II activities are mostly productive and feature work with collocations and specific word usage. These activities can also include work with register, associations, connotations, and learner dictionaries.

STEP II VOCABULARY ACTIVITIES: Sentence Level

Word Form Chart			
Noun	Verb	Adjective	Adverb
transformation	transform	transformative	....

D. Answer these questions in your notebook. Use each form of *transform* at least once in your answers. Refer to Reading 1 for information. Compare sentences with a partner.

1. What is the most significant way Earth's landmasses have changed since the days of Pangaea?
2. As scientific thinking became more advanced in Europe, how did explanations of Earth's geology change?
3. How did continental drift affect Antarctica?
4. What role did the theory of plate tectonics play in the debate about continental movement?
5. What big change is likely in the arrangement of Earth's continents?

NOTE

Each unit ends with topics and projects that teachers can use to take the lesson further. This section includes class discussion topics, online research projects, and essay ideas.

GOING UNDERGROUND

In this unit, you will

- ➲ read about the uses of underground space in two different places.
- ➲ learn to preview a reading and predict some ideas it might contain.
- ➲ increase your understanding of the target academic words for this unit:

assume	environment	liberal	predict	technique
create	ethnic	locate	similar	unique
emerge	immigrate	notwithstanding	structure	

SELF-ASSESSMENT OF TARGET WORDS

Learning a word is a gradual process.

- First, you learn to *recognize* the word. This means you know something about its spelling, pronunciation, and meanings.
- Next, you learn to *use* the word. This requires that you understand its spelling, pronunciation, grammar, and much more.

When you truly know a word, you can both recognize it and use it accurately.

Think carefully about how well you know each target word in this unit. They are listed in the objectives box, above. Then, write each word in the appropriate column in this chart.

I have never seen the word before.	I have seen the word but am not sure what it means.	I understand the word when I see or hear it in a sentence.	I have tried to use the word, but I am not sure I am using it correctly.	I use the word with confidence in either speaking *or* writing.	I use the word with confidence, both in speaking *and* writing.

BEFORE YOU READ

Read these questions. Discuss your answers in a small group.

1. Where is Australia? What do you know about its weather and its landscape?

2. Have you ever seen a movie or a photograph showing a mine? If so, describe what you saw. If not, what do you think conditions in a mine are like?

3. Would you like to live in an underground house? Why or why not?

READING STRATEGY: Previewing and Predicting

Previewing and *predicting* are strategies you can use before you read a text. A quick preview of the key elements of a text can help you predict what it might be about. This will help prepare you to take in the information as you read.

To preview a text:

- Read the title and any headings
- Look at any photographs, illustrations, or graphics.

Then, based on your preview, predict some ideas and information you expect to find in the text.

Take one minute to preview Reading 1. In the first column of the chart, write five words or phrases that caught your attention during your preview. Use each to create a prediction about the reading, in the middle column.

Word or phrase	Prediction	Accurate?
1. Down under	The reading will be about Australia.	

After you read, write *Y* next to each accurate prediction and *N* next to each inaccurate prediction in the last column of the chart. Write a question mark (?) if you are not sure. Discuss your results with the class.

This newspaper article is about a town in Australia's Outback, or isolated rural areas, where underground homes are common.

Coober Pedy: Really Down Under

Coober Pedy, a dusty town in South Australia, sits atop the world's greatest known deposits of opal—a milky white gem with veins and flecks of color. In hopes of striking it rich, gemstone
5 miners endure the harsh Outback **environment**. They suffer through dust storms, flies, and midsummer temperatures higher than 120° Fahrenheit (about 50° Celsius). To escape the heat and the flies, the people of Coober Pedy
10 go underground. They carve homes—called "dug-outs"—into the hills overlooking the town. Subterranean[1] living has become normal in Coober Pedy. There are shops, hotels, churches, and restaurants underground.

A dug-out home

15 **The miners arrive**

The first opals in Coober Pedy were discovered by a 14-year-old boy, Willie Hutchinson, who was looking for gold with his father in 1915. Many soldiers returning from
20 World War I came to the area and dug the first underground residences. A settlement took shape, which Aborigines (the original inhabitants of the area) called *Kupa Piti*, meaning "White Man's Burrow."

25 Most miners arrived in the 1960s and 1970s, **immigrating** to Australia and Coober Pedy from around the globe. The current population of 3,500 includes members of more than 40 **ethnic** or national groups, including Greeks, Poles,
30 Germans, Italians, Serbs, and Croats. They live together in relative harmony, producing 80 percent of the world's opal. Dealers from Hong Kong buy the opals directly from the miners because large companies cannot mine
35 here. Mining permits are sold only to individuals or small groups.

Rough edges

Like many mining communities, Coober Pedy is a rough and rugged town. Trucks with
40 "Explosives" signs on their sides clatter[2] around the streets. A sign outside the drive-in movie theater politely asks patrons not to bring in any dynamite. Card games turn into three-day activities, and mining disputes are settled with
45 fistfights in the pubs. The community takes a **liberal** attitude toward this behavior. After all, miners will be miners.

Its rough edges **notwithstanding**, Coober Pedy has a warmth and raw charm. Many
50 residents claim that long ago they stopped off only for gasoline and never left. Some fell in love with the **unique** (though sometimes scary) scenery. Just outside town are colorful rocky outcrops, used as the **location** for numerous
55 films including *Red Planet* and *Mad Max Beyond Thunderdome*. All around, the dry land forms a moonscape[3] cut through by fencing, which keeps

---

[1] *subterranean*: underground, from the Latin *sub*, meaning "under," and *terra*, meaning "land"
[2] *clatter*: make noise, such as when metal pieces repeatedly hit each other
[3] *moonscape*: a view of the surface of the moon

wild dogs out of the sheep-farming country to the south and east.

60   Tourism is flourishing, and unlucky miners have opened opal shops, cafés, and underground motels. Still, this is a working town, and tourists had better watch their step. Peter Rowe, formerly the head of the Mine Rescue Squad,
65 pulled plenty of dead and broken bodies out of mine shafts[4] during his career. The dirt tracks that cross the opal fields have many warning signs. Tourists have died after carelessly walking backwards while taking photographs. If the
70 holes don't get you, the monster trucks will.

Home is where the dirt is

    To **create** a typical dug-out, you need a hill and a drill. Most home-diggers tunnel into a hillside, which is a lot easier than digging
75 straight down. If the hill doesn't have a side of exposed rock, bulldozers push sand and loose soil away until a sandstone face **emerges**. Dug-outs in the 1980s, before Coober Pedy established a town government, were usually
80 blasted into a hillside, not actually dug. Drilling, with huge rigs meant to bore tunnels through mountains, is now the **technique** of choice.

    The homes are essentially artificial caves, but don't **assume** there is anything primitive about
85 them. Three-bedroom plans are common, and having your cave drilled out costs about the same as building a new above-ground home of similar size. Needless to say, the **structure** is solid, which creates some challenges. Electrical
90 wiring has to be placed in grooves in the rock and then plastered over. Plumbing is set in **similar** grooves.

---

[4] *shaft*: vertical tunnel or deep hole

Interior of a dug-out

    The hills inside the town limits were all claimed soon after the comforts of dug-out
95 living became well known. Coober Pedy had to expand, not because it needed more space but because it needed more hills. Some town planners **predict** that Coober Pedy will sprawl out to great distances as more miners seek a
100 place to burrow. Some paved roads have been laid, most of them running along the faces of the hills and out to mine shafts. A lot more will be needed if homeowners head to the far-flung hills.

    One home, a comfortable dug-out near
105 the Serbian Orthodox church, illustrates the advantages of underground living. Outside, it is pushing 104° Fahrenheit (40° Celsius). This is relatively mild for January in Coober Pedy, but hot nonetheless. Inside, it is blessedly cool.
110 The low ceiling and honey-colored stone walls give a feeling of safety and refuge. Area rugs and comfortable furniture soften the interior. Appliances are set into custom-carved nooks. Hole sweet hole.

READING COMPREHENSION

Mark each sentence as *T* (true) or *F* (false) according to the information in Reading 1. Use the dictionary to help you understand new words.

.... 1. Underground homes are considered normal in Coober Pedy.

.... 2. The first underground homes in Coober Pedy were built by Aborigines.

.... 3. All the opals located in and near Coober Pedy belong to one trading company.

.... 4. Coober Pedy has liberal laws about drinking and gambling.

.... 5. The environment around Coober Pedy is dry and rocky.

.... 6. Some tourists have died from falling into holes in the town.

.... 7. Most underground structures in Coober Pedy were originally opal mines.

.... 8. The cost of creating an underground home is similar to the cost of building a home on the surface.

.... 9. It is easier to dig an underground home into a hillside than into the ground.

.... 10. So far, only one underground home in Coober Pedy has water service.

STEP I VOCABULARY ACTIVITIES: Word Level

A. Read these excerpts from another article on underground homes. For each excerpt, cross out the one word or phrase in parentheses with a different meaning from the other three choices. Compare answers with a partner.

1. Unlike most homes, underground homes can be (*located / built / ~~structured~~ / positioned*) on steep surfaces. They take up very little surface space.

2. Underground building (*methods / houses / techniques / processes*) mostly use materials already available at the home site.

3. A typical house makes (*careful / wide / extensive / liberal*) use of energy, mostly for heating and cooling. An underground home needs little or no heating or cooling, because underground temperatures remain stable. Consequently, it uses only about 20% of the energy used in a conventional home.

4. Underground (*environments / settings / surroundings / creations*) provide excellent noise insulation. Underground homes are exceptionally quiet places to live.

5. Finally, underground houses have a (*special / well-known / unique / one-of-a-kind*) ability to blend in with nature. This not only looks nice but also preserves habitat for wildlife.

The word *notwithstanding* means "not being prevented by" or "not preventing." It can come before a noun phrase (*Notwithstanding* the rain, the players finished the game) or after one (The rain *notwithstanding*, the players finished the game).

B. Read each pair of sentences. Put a check (✓) next to the ones that can be made into one sentence using *notwithstanding*, then, write the sentences. Compare answers in a small group. Discuss what connectors (*because, therefore, yet,* etc.) you could use for the other sentences.

.... **1.** Coober Pedy is known for its uncomfortable heat and dryness. People like living there.

.... **2.** Building a dug-out is a great challenge. More and more miners want underground homes.

.... **3.** A system of roads out to the hills is under development. Many people are planning to build underground homes there.

.... **4.** Tourism is flourishing in Coober Pedy. There are many shops, cafés, and motels.

.... **5.** Tourists sometimes have accidents in Coober Pedy. Signs tell them to be careful.

.... **6.** The people of Coober Pedy come from more than 40 ethnic groups. They work together very well.

STEP II VOCABULARY ACTIVITIES: Sentence Level

Word Form Chart			
Noun	Verb	Adjective	Adverb
prediction	predict	predictable predicted	predictably

To *predict* something means to "say something is likely to happen in the future."

Town planners **predict** *that in the next few years, more people will want underground homes.*

Predict is also often used to talk about weather.

Forecasters are **predicting** *another hot day tomorrow.*

C. Answer these questions in your notebook. Use the form of *predict* in parentheses. Compare sentences with a partner. Refer to Reading 1 for information.

1. You want to buy 100 opals. What can you guess about their origins? (*predict*)

I can predict that about 80 of them will be from Coober Pedy.

2. Why do people in Coober Pedy not get upset about fights and other rough behavior? (*predictable*)

3. What would the weather service normally say about tomorrow's weather in Coober Pedy? (*predict*)

4. Someone is planning to construct an underground home in Coober Pedy. What tools will he or she probably use? (*prediction*)

5. Imagine that people do not build a large number of homes in the hills far from town. In that case, what could you say about the development of Coober Pedy's road system? (*predicted*)

Word Form Chart			
Noun	Verb	Adjective	Adverb
assumption	assume	assumed	....
creation creator creativity	create	creative	creatively
emergence	emerge	emergent	....
similarity	....	similar	similarly
structure	structure	structural	structurally

D. Read these sentences about underground structures. Then, in your notebook, restate each of the sentences using the words in parentheses. Do not change the meanings of the sentences. Be prepared to read aloud or discuss your sentences in class.

1. Underground homes may or may not be safe. Anyone who is planning to live in one should check it carefully. (*assume*)

   Anyone planning to live in an underground home should not just assume it is safe but should check it carefully.

2. The roof of a dug-out could collapse if there are not enough walls in the underground space to support it. (*structure, structural,* or *structurally*)

3. A harmful gas called radon is naturally present in most soil, and it slowly makes its way into underground spaces. (*emergence* or *emerge*)

4. Since rainwater naturally flows downward from the ground, people who live underground have to expect water problems. (*assumption* or *assume*)

5. When designing an air-circulation system for a home underground, a builder has to think flexibly and imaginatively. (*creative*)

6. Too much moisture and not enough fresh air can make an underground home moldy, like a pile of wet clothes. (*similarly* or *similar*)

BEFORE YOU READ

Read these questions. Discuss your answers in a small group.

1. Have you ever been in a tunnel, an underpass, a cave, or some other space underground? Was it uncomfortable or frightening? Why or why not?

2. If you dug a hole in your neighborhood, what do you think you would find at various depths — 6 inches, 2 feet, 10 feet, and 50 feet?

3. Why do cities put water pipes, gas pipes, electric lines, and other utility equipment underground instead of aboveground?

READING STRATEGY

Preview the reading by looking at the title, the headings, and the photos. Based on your preview, what do you think the reading is about? Write your prediction(s). Then compare your prediction(s) with a partner.

....

....

....

READ

This reading examines the underground systems on which the city of Philadelphia (Philly) depends.

Understanding Philly's Basement

Strolling down Philadelphia's city sidewalks, we assume we are walking on solid earth. In reality, just beneath our feet is a vast, dark, and complex environment—water pipes, sewers full
5 of smelly waste, electrical wires, and television cables. There are also tunnels, abandoned subway stations, graves, hidden waterways, archaeological sites, mines, and more.

Sometimes, one of these underground
10 structures fails. A small break in a pipe can eventually create a sinkhole that swallows whatever stood above it. On June 28, two cars fell 70 feet when an enormous sinkhole appeared on Route 924, north of Pottsville,
15 Pennsylvania. That same day, two truckers were killed after their rigs fell into a sinkhole on Interstate 99 in New York State.

An underground mystery

So just how bad are things down there in
20 lower Philadelphia? The answer is simple and frightening: We don't know.

Philadelphia was carefully planned out by William Penn, who established the city in 1682. The orderly Mr. Penn obviously had
25 little influence below the surface. The city's underground has been built, liberally expanded,

A car falls into a sinkhole

and repaired in no particular order for 300 years. Some underground work was never documented. For example, in the mid-1800s, anti-slavery groups hid escaped slaves in secret shelters belowground to keep them from being kidnapped and returned to the South. In the past, various ethnic groups in the city were sometimes fearful or suspicious of city authorities. They built underground meeting rooms, storehouses, and even treasure vaults for their communities.

A tunnel under Philadelphia

Even if records were kept, they may be of no help. Many have been scattered or lost, or were simply inaccurate to begin with. This matters for many reasons. The most important is that new systems are hard to plan unless you know where the old ones are. And then there are sinkholes. Until we figure out exactly what is where, we cannot predict where the next man-eating hole might develop.

Mapping the depths

"Philadelphia is an old city," says Lucio Soibelman, an associate professor of civil and environmental engineering at Carnegie Mellon University, "so you have old infrastructure[1] and new infrastructure. You have new pipes that are being mapped with GIS (geographic information systems) technology and you have old things that no one knows are there. This is not something that was designed in a perfect way. There's a lot going on, and a lot of research is needed to find out what is underground."

The most common technique for finding buried pipes or cables is to use a kind of metal detector. The problem is that many underground utilities aren't metal. Many gas pipes are plastic. The channels of the sewer system are lined with baked clay or plastic. Because of this, most glass fiber optic cables and many newer nonmetallic pipes contain "tracer wires" that can be picked up by metal detectors. Older pipes, however, remain invisible.

Ground penetrating radar (GPR) is an important new tool. In a way, it is similar to the sonar systems used to find objects under water. GPR sends thousands of radar pulses per second into the ground. The signals are then either absorbed or reflected back to a receiver. Software senses how long it takes the GPR signals to bounce back. Differences of even a nanosecond in bounce-back time will be registered. A software-generated image of what lies beneath the surface soon emerges on the receiver's screen.

An underground mystery unique to Philadelphia was finally unraveled in 2005 by using GPR. An escape tunnel under Eastern State Penitentiary in the Fairmount neighborhood was used in 1945 by a group of twelve prisoners. Their ingenious tunneling notwithstanding, they were all easily recaptured in the city. They had left trails of underground mud as they tried to hide. Authorities knew where the tunnel started, but they didn't know until the GPR readings exactly where it went. The detection of other abandoned tunnels is important to law-enforcement authorities. Such underground passageways could be used by persons trying to immigrate illegally through Philly's seaport. Smugglers[2] or even terrorists could also find them useful. The police want to know where they are, and GPR is a big help.

---

[1] *infrastructure*: the basic structures and systems of a city or country, such as roads, sewers, etc.

[2] *smuggler*: a person who takes goods in or out of a place illegally and in secret

Robots that can patrol large water systems are another great innovation. They are already used in other cities. In Pittsburgh, for example, a robotic system called Responder travels inside sewers, operated by a remote control, looking for problems in the pipes. Responder is equipped with laser and sonar sensors that scan the insides of pipe walls. The slightest bit of corrosion or the smallest leak will register. Advanced software can then construct extremely detailed 3-D models of the pipe walls.

OK. Now what?

Locating problems is important, but it's not enough. Fixing them is the bulk of the job. Fixing and updating underground utilities in a city is very complicated. It's not just a matter of digging a hole, pulling out bad pipes, and installing good ones. The city and its neighborhoods must continue functioning during the many months it takes to put things right.

A company named Insituform has developed technology that can fix a pipe from the inside before it breaks, without any digging. They fill a tube with a special kind of resin (a sticky substance), turn it inside out, and send it through the pipe. Then, they heat the water inside the pipe. The resin expands outward, attaches to the interior surface of the pipe, and then hardens. This creates a new pipe inside the old pipe.

The company actually used this technique on the sewers under one of the most famous buildings in the United States, the White House, in Washington, D.C. The pipes dated from around the time of the Civil War (mid 1800s) and needed extensive repair. For security reasons—and because it would look really ugly—the government decided not to dig up the lawn, but rather to work underground, and under tourists' feet.

READING COMPREHENSION

Mark each sentence as *T* (true) or *F* (false) according to the information in Reading 2. Use the dictionary to help you understand new words.

.... **1.** Philadelphia no longer locates pipes or cables underground.

.... **2.** The collapse of underground structures sometimes kills people traveling on the surface.

.... **3.** William Penn carefully planned Philadelphia's underground environment in the 1680s.

.... **4.** Some residents of Philadelphia today use underground structures to hide things from city officials.

.... **5.** Old infrastructure is easier to locate than new infrastructure.

.... **6.** GPR can detect even non-metal items.

.... **7.** By using GPR, the police easily recaptured twelve escaped prisoners.

.... **8.** Systems like Responder use radar or sonar to find out where old sewers are.

.... **9.** Robots can discover problems by looking at pipes from the inside.

.... **10.** The sewers under the White House were fixed by creating new pipes inside old ones.

STEP I VOCABULARY ACTIVITIES: Word Level

A. Complete the sentences about urban explorers (UEs), using the target vocabulary in the box. The synonyms in parentheses can help you.

assume	environment	notwithstanding	unique
emerge	liberal	similar to	

.... **a.** Perhaps because people are fascinated by hidden things, underground

spaces have always had a .... appeal to explorers.
(not found anywhere else)

.... **b.** Police often arrest UE groups as they .... from tunnels
(come out)

and charge them with trespassing. UE groups expect this and often

carry checks with them so they can bail themselves out of jail.

.... **c.** Urban explorers generally take a very .... approach

to property rights. As long as they aren't damaging anything, they
(unrestricted)

.... they have the right to use the property.
(believe)

.... **d.** MIT was only one of several hot spots for UEs. Informal groups

.... the MIT group explored the undergrounds of
(like)
Paris, Toronto, and Sydney.

.... **e.** Starting in the 1970s, a movement called "urban exploration"

(UE) took special notice of rarely visited parts of the underground

.... , like tunnels, drains, and abandoned subway
(space)
stations.

.... **f.** Students at the Massachusetts Institute of Technology (MIT)

contributed greatly to the UE culture. .... the fact that
(despite)
it was illegal, they developed a tradition of exploring the steam tunnels

at the university.

B. Tell the story of urban exploration by putting the sentences in activity A into a logical order. Number them from _1_ to _6_ (more than one sequence may be possible). Then, use the target words as you compare stories with a partner.

Many English words have several related meanings. *Locate* is an example. All its meanings refer to "place," but in slightly different ways. A good dictionary will list these meanings for *locate* and its related forms.

C. Look up *locate* and its forms in your dictionary. Then read these sample sentences and answer the questions that follow. Compare answers with a partner.

a. On my first day in the new office, I tried to **locate** all the fire exits on my floor.
b. After looking at several cities, Caitlin decided to **relocate** to Chicago.
c. To ensure privacy, it is best to **locate** trees and bushes between your house and your neighbor's house.
d. The university has a beautiful **location** on the shores of Lake Martin.

1. Put a check (✓) next to the word closest in meaning to *locate*. Look up each choice in your dictionary before you answer.

    .... situate   .... move   .... inhabit   .... clear

2. Sentences a, b, and c show three slightly different meanings of the verb *locate*. Write the letter of the sentence next to the correct meaning.

    .... to set up a home or business in a new place

    .... to search for and find something

    .... to put something into a place

3. Look at the sample sentences in your dictionary for *locate* and its forms. What is being located in each of those samples?

    ....

    ....

    ....

4. Put a check (✓) next to each real meaning of *location*. (Not every item should be checked.) Confirm your choices with your dictionary.

    .... moving from one place to another

    .... a place where a movie is filmed

    .... finding where something is

    .... a point of view on a political issue

    .... a site

STEP II VOCABULARY ACTIVITIES: Sentence Level

To *assume* something is to believe it without checking whether it is true. Our assumptions are reflected in what we do and how we see the world. For example, you probably assume that a person wearing a police uniform is a police officer.

D. In each of these situations, at least one assumption lies behind the action. Identify one assumption for each action and write it in the middle column. In the last column, write *yes* or *no* to indicate whether you would also make this assumption. Be ready to discuss your answers with a partner.

Action	Assumption	Yes/No
A customer goes to a bank and gives a teller several thousand dollars to deposit.		
A student tells her deepest thoughts and secrets to her best friend.		
A football player walks alone at night through a very rough part of town.		
On the highway, someone drives at speeds slightly over the speed limit.		

E. Incorrect assumptions can be embarrassing or even dangerous. Rank these (possibly) incorrect assumptions from *1* (most dangerous) to *6* (least dangerous).

.... If someone mentions a doctor, he or she is referring to a man, not a woman.

.... The government always does what is best for the nation.

.... It doesn't matter what your grades are, as long as you finish school.

.... The groceries I buy have been officially inspected, so they're safe.

.... If I tell someone a secret, he or she won't tell it to other people.

.... Car accidents only happen to other people, not to me.

As a class, make a chart and tally everyone's answers. Which assumption does the class consider most dangerous? Least dangerous? Why do you think this is true?

F. Discuss these questions in a small group. Use the dictionary to clarify word meanings, if needed.

1. In which environment would an underground house be hardest to build? Why?

   a. a tropical rainforest   **c.** Antarctica

   b. New York City   **d.** a desert

2. Think about a town or city you know well. Which of these structures or services does it have underground? Who owns them? Why were they put underground?

   a. homes   **c.** sewers

   b. tunnels   **d.** electrical lines

G. Look at these arguments for and against urban exploration. Restate each idea in your notebook, using the word in parentheses. Then, write a paragraph that expresses your own opinion. Try to use as many target words as possible in your work. Be prepared to read aloud or discuss your paragraph in class.

For	Against
Serious urban explorers cause no damage to the structures they explore. Their rule is, "Take only pictures. Leave only footprints." (*assume*)	Not every urban explorer is harmless. Some steal from the places they enter. Others spray graffiti there. (*assume*)
Although some underground spaces are dangerous, urban explorers can prepare themselves well. They are ready for dangers like steam explosions or live electrical wires. (*predict*)	Old tunnels and other underground spaces could contain dozens of dangers, from toxic chemicals to collapsing roofs. No one knows what is there. And no explorer can protect himself from the most serious ones, like steam explosions. (*predict*)
There is a law that says that a member of the general public has the right to use abandoned property as long as he or she doesn't damage it. (*location*)	Urban explorers do not have any right to enter restricted underground spaces. This is trespassing—being in a place without the permission of its owner—and it is illegal. (*location*)

H. Self-Assessment Review: Go back to page 1 and reassess your knowledge of the target vocabulary. How has your understanding of the words changed? What words do you feel most comfortable with now?

WRITING AND DISCUSSION TOPICS

1. Aboveground houses are attractive for some reasons. Underground houses are attractive for other reasons. Which would you prefer to live in, and why?

2. Reading 1 says rough behavior, such as fistfights in pubs, is generally tolerated in Coober Pedy. Is this tolerance a good thing? Should the town adopt stricter rules? What might happen if the town did try to reduce this kind of behavior?

3. Much of Reading 2 is about Philadelphia's efforts simply to find underground systems. If you were planning a new city, what could you do to make sure your city would not face a problem like Philadelphia's? Be specific about the procedures or equipment you would use.

4. Some structures or systems are placed underground for security reasons. For example, an underground water system is less likely to be poisoned than one aboveground. Describe some ways in which an underground location provides better security than an aboveground location.

5. Reading 2 describes several techniques for finding and fixing underground systems. These are not perfect, so better techniques and equipment are continually being developed. Try to predict improvements that might occur within the next 20 years. What equipment will probably be developed? What will it be used for? Make your predictions as realistic as possible.

THE BUSINESS OF BRANDING

In this unit, you will

- ➲ read about the branding of products and its importance for business.
- ➲ learn to identify main ideas and kinds of support in a text.
- ➲ increase your understanding of the target academic words for this unit:

consume	corporate	label	register	symbol
contradict	equate	medium	revenue	theme
convert	finance	presume	subsidy	

SELF-ASSESSMENT OF TARGET WORDS

Think carefully about how well you know each target word in this unit. Then, write it in the appropriate column in the chart.

I have never seen the word before.	I have seen the word but am not sure what it means.	I understand the word when I see or hear it in a sentence.	I have tried to use the word, but I am not sure I am using it correctly.	I use the word with confidence in either speaking *or* writing.	I use the word with confidence, both in speaking *and* writing.

MORE WORDS YOU'LL NEED

blog: a Web log, a personal website on which someone expresses opinions or gives personal information

subculture: a set of activities, objects, and beliefs associated with a group within a larger culture

BEFORE YOU READ

Read these questions. Discuss your answers in a small group.

1. Think about some basic products you buy (toothpaste, soft drinks, etc.). What brands are they? Try to list at least five products for which you usually choose the same brands.

2. Why do people often buy the same brand?

3. In your opinion, what is the highest-quality brand of car in the world? Why do you think so?

READ

This article is about the influence that a brand can have on its customers and their culture.

The Power of Branding

1   Let's say your company has been making athletic shoes for 50 or 60 years. They are good shoes. Nevertheless, other companies have sped past you in the race for fame and the **revenue** that goes with it. Products with the logos of the other companies are status **symbols**. Products with your logo make people think of basketball stars from the 1970s. To turn things around, you have to **convert** your product's old-fashioned image into something new, and make sure **consumers** get the message. They must **equate** your product with some larger idea that has nothing to do with[1] shoes—beauty, prosperity, or even world peace. In other words, you have to build a brand.

From the ranch to Rolls Royce

2   The term *brand* comes from the practice of using a hot iron to burn a distinctive mark into the skin of a cow or a horse. For example, the owner of the Double Jay Ranch might brand a "JJ" mark on his stock. This brand helps the rancher distinguish his or her animals from others. The brand is a kind of **label**, a device for creating recognition. Branding on products is also all about recognition.

3   People equate the name *Rolls Royce*, for example, with classic luxury. The recognition value of this brand is enormous. It even **registers** with people who have never seen one of the company's cars. When the German company BMW bought the Rolls company in 1998, they were careful to change nothing. They continued to build cars in Greenwood, England, because Rolls Royce is thought of as British. Not even BMW—a powerful brand itself—has the same aristocratic image. Rolls Royce turned 100 years old in 2004, and the brand continues to use the **themes** of integrity, dependability, and even Britishness in its advertising.

---

[1] *have nothing to do with*: not be related to or connected to

Rolls Royce drivers and NASCAR

4 As the story of Rolls Royce shows, an extremely successful brand may become an enduring part of a culture. When that happens to a brand with a worldwide presence, the company may get **contradictory** results. In its home culture, the brand may benefit from being a sort of national treasure; however, it may suffer overseas from being a symbol of foreignness. The McDonald's restaurant franchise offers just one prominent case of a corporation fighting to guide its brand through these difficult waters.

5 Subcultures can form around a certain brand. NASCAR (the National Association for Stock Car Auto Racing) is in business to organize auto races and sell related products, but its brand is about much more than that. NASCAR was founded in the late 1940s and originally built its image around beachside racing in Daytona, Florida. It revised its brand through the 1980s and 1990s to appeal to a broader audience. Nearly 75 million Americans now consider themselves part of a NASCAR subculture.

6 Because NASCAR has a connection to such a large segment of the population, it is a **medium** in itself. It can **finance** many of its operations by, for instance, allowing its name to appear on products and selling advertising space alongside its racetracks.

My brand, myself

7 Among some strong brands, the line between promotional and personal image is unclear. Some customers may adopt a brand's image as their own image. The ads for Nike shoes show no-nonsense athletes. A customer might buy Nike shoes because she considers herself a no-nonsense athlete—and she wants others to **presume** this, too.

8 Biker subculture in the United States owes a great deal to the branding success of the Harley-Davidson motorcycle company. Its American-manufactured motorbikes are promoted as a symbol of patriotism. Harley has also managed to turn its motorcycles into symbols of opposition to mainstream[2] cultural values. In a radio interview, Harley-Davidson's CEO, Jim Ziemer, points out one way his brand—and its black-and-orange logo—has become very personal.

> **Interviewer:** When business school students study branding, one of the names that's always at the top of that list is Harley Davidson. I'd like you to tell me, first of all, in your mind, what is it that makes a brand?
>
> **Ziemer:** A brand is made when a person really feels a connection with that brand. I mean, we've taken it to the ultimate, where a lot of our customers have a [Harley-Davidson] tattoo on their body so they really feel very special and connected with the brand.

The origins of branding, the hot irons and the Double Jay, seem not so far away.

---

[2] *mainstream*: representing the way most people in a culture think or behave

READING COMPREHENSION

Mark each sentence as *T* (true) or *F* (false) according to the information in Reading 1. Use the dictionary to help you understand new words.

.... 1. Branding is the process of equating a product with an idea or image.

.... 2. Ranchers brand animals by burning marks into their skin.

.... 3. Rolls Royce is no longer a British corporation.

.... 4. The Rolls Royce brand has lost revenue because it is associated with old things.

.... 5. In many countries, people don't like to buy products with foreign brand names.

.... 6. NASCAR is a political organization that has created a brand.

.... 7. People often presume a person fits the image of a brand because he or she uses the brand's product.

.... 8. Harley-Davidson motorcycles are manufactured outside the United States.

.... 9. The Harley-Davidson brand is associated with classic luxury.

.... 10. Some people have Harley-Davidson symbols tattooed on their skin.

READING STRATEGY: Finding the Main Idea

The main ideas in Reading 1 appear as "chunks," and the different chunks are separated by headings. A chunk may consist of one paragraph or several paragraphs. Recognizing these chunks can help you see relationships between main ideas and details.

A. Use the list of phrases to identify the main idea of each chunk in Reading 1. Then, circle the paragraph number(s) to indicate which paragraph(s) make up the chunk.

branding as a tool for recognition
brands and one's self-image
brands as part of culture
why companies build brands

Chunk 1 ......*why companies build brands*...... ① 2 3 4 5 6 7 8

Chunk 2 .... 1 2 3 4 5 6 7 8

Chunk 3 .... 1 2 3 4 5 6 7 8

Chunk 4 .... 1 2 3 4 5 6 7 8

One way writers support a main idea is by giving examples. You can often find phrases in a text that signal examples. Here are some common signals for examples in a text:

for example...   like...   one way...

for instance...   such as...   to illustrate...

B. Complete the table by identifying the examples in Reading 1. Write the signals, the examples, and tell what they are examples of.

Paragraph	Signal	Example	An example of...
Paragraph 2	*for example*	*the Double Jay brand*	*the branding of animals*
Paragraph 4			
Paragraph 6			
Paragraph 8			

STEP I VOCABULARY ACTIVITIES: Word Level

A. Read these excerpts from another article about branding. For each excerpt, cross out the one word or phrase in parentheses with a different meaning from the other three choices. Compare answers with a partner.

1. A team from a university in Germany has found that the (*symbols / revenues / logos / labels*) of popular brands activated parts of the brain linked to self-identity and reward.

2. The researchers used magnetic resonance imaging (MRI) to study the brain activity of 20 men and women looking at the brand logos of insurance companies and car manufacturers. Then they (*converted / compared / matched / related*) the MRI data to maps that show specific regions of the brain.

3. They discovered that well-known brands activated parts of the brain associated with positive emotions, self-identity, and reward. Less well-known brands (*registered with / made an impression on / had an effect on / harmed*) parts of the brain associated with negative emotional responses.

4. He said, "Marketing is all about learning by association. (*Companies / Corporations / Departments / Firms*) constantly push the same image over and over again from a variety of media."

5. "So people (*associate / equate / connect / reward*) a famous brand with positive imagery, and you would expect that positive imagery to produce positive emotional responses."

As an adjective, the word *medium* refers to anything that is not large and not small, but somewhere between, as in "a person of medium height."

As a noun, however, *medium* has a completely different meaning. It refers to a way to convey or send something. The plural form is *media*.

*Some chemical reactions require a **medium** to help them happen.*

*Television and radio are popular **media** for getting the news.*

B. What is each of these things a medium for? List as many things as you can. Discuss your ideas with a partner.

1. a newspaper: ....

2. the telephone system: ....

3. a letter: ....

4. the postal service: ....

5. the Internet: ....

6. gossip: ....

The verb *subsidize* means "to give money to someone or an organization to help pay for something." The noun is *subsidy*.

*The city **subsidizes** ambulance companies in order to keep the price of their services low.*

*These companies could not continue to operate without **subsidies** from the city.*

C. Read these pairs of items. With a partner, write down some ways that the first item might subsidize the second. Then, in a small group, discuss whether you think the subsidies should exist or should continue. Give reasons for your opinions.

1. parent/child's education: ....

2. government/students: ....

3. government/small businesses: ....

4. employer/employee's healthcare: ....

5. employer/employee's education: ....

6. local government/rent: ....

Word Form Chart			
Noun	Verb	Adjective	Adverb
consumption consumer	consume	consumable	....
corporation	incorporate	corporate	....
presumption	presume	presumable presumed	presumably
symbol symbolism	symbolize	symbolic	symbolically
theme	....	thematic	thematically

D. Read these excerpts from another article about branding. Then, in your notebook, restate the essential information, using the words in parentheses. Focus on main ideas and leave out unnecessary details. Be prepared to read aloud or discuss your sentences in class.

1. Your first big decision should be: How will you get your brand out to the public? (*consumer*)

2. If you decide to advertise, first decide what role the ads will play in your business development plan. (*corporate*)

3. What idea do you want your products to represent? How will they represent it? (*symbolize*)

4. Is your goal in advertising to promote name awareness? One insurance company, AFLAC, uses a duck in all their ads. The duck appears in different situations where a person might need insurance and quacks "AFLAC." Now, 90% of Americans recognize the company's name. (*theme*)

5. Test your ad ideas before you spend money on them. Teens are especially hard to target. They chew up images in a few weeks and go on looking for the next meal. (*consume*)

6. To illustrate this point, the government once spent $929 million on an anti-drug campaign targeted at teens. They thought the ads would be very powerful, but they didn't test them on teens. After the ads started running, they discovered that kids ignored them. (*presumed*)

Some verbs *collocate* with—often occur with—certain prepositions. These sets of words are called *collocations*. Here are some examples of collocations for target words in this unit:

convert to/into	*A transformer **converts** one type of electric current **into** another.*
equate with	*Teenagers often **equate** unusual clothes **with** personal freedom.*
register with	*I don't like this ad. The images just don't **register with** me.*
finance by/with	*Youth sports programs **finance** their activities **by** selling tickets.*
	*They **finance** their activities **with** the revenue from ticket sales.*

E. Answer these questions in your notebook, using the verb in parentheses. Be sure to use a preposition that collocates with it. Refer to Reading 1 for information. Compare answers with a partner.

1. Why are symbols like the Rolls Royce badge or the Harley-Davidson logo so powerful? (*register*)

2. Why does a weak brand harm the sales of a product? (*equate*)

3. How do the license fees for NASCAR's name help the organization? (*finance*)

4. Why would a stronger brand help the shoe company mentioned in Paragraph 1 of the reading? (*convert*)

READING 2

BEFORE YOU READ

Read these questions. Discuss your answers in a small group.

1. Name some smaller groups within the society where you live—your class, your school, or even your generation. What makes these small groups different from others?

2. Do you look for brand names when you shop for clothes, or do brands not matter to you? Do you usually buy clothes of a few certain brands? Why?

3. How do young people often make themselves different from their parents? With clothes? Music? Other things?

READ

This reading looks at brands as an instrument of youth culture and self-expression.

My Brand Is Me

Aaron Bondaroff is 29. A-Ron, as he is also known, has a very high opinion of his own importance in the youth culture of Lower Manhattan in New York. As far as he is
5 concerned, you can presume that every cool person south of Delancey Street will like what he likes. No need to ask them what they want. Ask him. A-Ron has been asking himself a question lately: "How do I turn my lifestyle into
10 a business?"

Bondaroff dropped out of high school at age 15 to live a wild life and hang out with the people who were worth hanging out with. He got a job in Lower Manhattan at a store selling
15 items with the "Supreme" name on them. Theoretically a skateboard brand, Supreme was really a brand about attitude. In his store, clerks would insult you to your face if you weren't cool enough. A-Ron was not only cool enough, he was
20 photographed for Supreme ads and became its "unofficial face." Supreme caught on in Japan. By the time Bondaroff was 21, he was visiting Tokyo and getting asked for autographs by kids who had seen his picture in magazines. They weren't
25 exactly sure who he was. They just equated his image with fame and style. One fan called him the guy who "gets famous for doing nothing."

While still working a retail job, he was also making a business out of being a cool guy. A
30 group in Australia paid for him to come there to discuss new trends. His elaborate birthday party was **subsidized** by Nike. He was figuring out that he had the option of becoming a "culture expert." He concluded that there was no reason
35 to rent his coolness to other companies. If they could earn revenue from his great taste, he figured, he could earn even more.

Young people have always found fresh ways to rebel, express individuality, or form
40 subculture communities: new art, new music, new literature, new films, new forms of leisure, or even whole new media forms. A-Ron's preferred form of expression, however, is none of those things. He calls it "aNYthing". He talks
45 about it as something bold, radical, and anti-big business. He makes it sound like some very hip independent film company or a punk band. In fact, aNYthing is just a brand. A-Ron puts the label on T-shirts, hats, and other items, which he
50 sells in his own store, among other places.

Part of the aNYthing product line

This might seem strange, since most of us think of branding as a thoroughly **corporate** practice. It's what huge companies do, and it involves financial assets in the tens of millions.
55 After all, a 30-second TV ad can cost as much as $2.5 million.

Branding is both simpler and more complicated than that. It is basically the process of attaching an idea to a product. The item for
60 sale becomes the symbol of an attractive quality or idea. Decades ago that idea might have been trustworthiness, effectiveness, or reasonable price—qualities that related directly to the product. Over time, the ideas have become
65 more abstract. Branding persuades people to consume the idea by consuming the product. In its modern form, branding ties a product not to one idea but to an entire theme, such as

nonconformity[1] or achievement. A strong brand becomes a form of identity.

Of course, companies don't go into business to express a particular point of view. They have stuff to sell, and this has nothing to do with beliefs or ideals. We all know that corporate branding is just a way to get our money. And that fact registers with cool, street-wise guys like A-Ron better than with anybody. Which is why it seems so contradictory to claim that a brand is rebellious. Branding is a form of personal expression? Independent businesses are a means of dropping out? Turning your lifestyle into a business is rebellious?

And yet thousands and thousands of young people are following in A-Ron's path. They are turned off by the world of shopping malls and big-box stores. They see alternative businesses as the perfect tool of protest. Some of these discontented young people design furniture and housewares or convert their handicraft hobbies into businesses. Others make toys or paint sneakers. Many of them see their businesses as not only *non*-corporate but also *anti*-corporate. They protest culture's materialism with their own style of materialism. In other words, they see products and brands as a medium for creative expression.

A-Ron has branded himself, but it is not a brand with a large range. How does your brand get bigger when it is, essentially, just you? He is tying aNYthing to more projects—music, books, even a documentary film. His blog announces the latest parties and offers pictures of the cool people dropping by his store. He has been thinking about whether he can open a store in Japan. He seems to think he can be to the world what he believes he is to Lower Manhattan.

---

[1] *nonconformity*: behavior or thinking that is different from most people in society

READING COMPREHENSION

Mark each sentence as *T* (true) or *F* (false) according to the information in Reading 2. Use the dictionary to help you understand new words.

.... **1.** A-Ron owns a corporation in New York City called "Supreme."

.... **2.** A-Ron presumes himself to be an expert on what young people like.

.... **3.** Companies have sent A-Ron to Japan and Australia so he can find out what is popular among young people there.

.... **4.** The brand name "aNYthing" is attached to a film company, a musical group, and clothing.

.... **5.** A-Ron wants his brand to symbolize opposing the power of large companies.

.... **6.** His earlier success has given A-Ron millions of dollars to promote his brand.

.... **7.** Brands today emphasize reliability and price less than brands of the past did.

.... **8.** A-Ron does not understand that companies use brands mostly to make money.

.... **9.** Alternative businesses are often set up to express a dislike of large corporations.

.... **10.** A-Ron has closed his store and now sells products only on the Internet.

READING STRATEGY

Read the details from Reading 2 in the box. Decide which main idea each detail is related to and write it in the appropriate column. Look back at Reading 2 if necessary. Discuss your answers with a partner.

a blog	materialism
A-Ron as a culture expert	music, books, and a documentary film
companies with stuff to sell	nonconformity or achievement
furniture shops	south of Delancey Street
labels on T-shirts	the cost of a TV ad

Who is A-Ron?

A-Ron as a culture expert

....

....

What is aNYthing?

....

....

....

How branding works

....

....

....

Products as a form of rebellion

....

....

....

STEP I VOCABULARY ACTIVITIES: Word Level

A. Complete the sentences about the movie *Wag the Dog* by using the target vocabulary in the box. Use each item one time. The synonyms in parentheses can help you.

consume	contradicting	convert
equate	media	presumes
register with	symbols	theme

1. In the 1997 comedy film *Wag the Dog*, advisers to the U.S. President make up a fake war so that a scandal involving the President will not .... *(get the attention of)* the public until after an election.

2. A Hollywood producer is hired to .... the abstract idea of a war *(turn)* into something the American public can see. Essentially, his job is to brand the war and sell it to America.

3. First, he finds ways to silence any .... arguments about the war *(opposing)* by building a powerful image machine. He has special songs written for the fake war and creates fake news reports in Hollywood film studios.

continued

4. The producer hires a team of specialists headed by "The Fad King." King's talent is knowing what Americans will .... and how to package it.
   (accept)

5. King's job is to sway public opinion to support the fake war. He invents .... and products to go along with the show.
   (signs)

6. For example, he .... Americans will wear armbands that are a specific shade of green, because that color was popular in cars the previous year.
   (believes)

7. King arranges for events to happen. The news .... accept these as real events, and soon the public believes them, too.
   (information distributors)

8. One .... of *Wag the Dog* is that, when expertly manipulated, the public is willing to .... brand images with reality. In the end, even though it is all fiction, the "war" is a success because it has a strong enough brand.
   (recurring idea)
   (think they are the same)

B. Read the sample sentences that feature forms of the word *convert*. Then, answer the questions that follow. Use your dictionary as suggested. Compare answers with a partner.

> **a.** In a process called friction, mechanical energy is *converted* into heat energy.
> **b.** The Environmental Coalition supports the *conversion* of old coal-burning power plants into modern plants.
> **c.** Late in life, Peter Mortenson became a *convert* to a religion called Pangeism.
> **d.** If you snap a set of wheels onto the blade, this ice skate is *convertible* into a roller skate.

1. In the sample sentences in the box, what is converted in each case? What is it converted into?

   a. .... into ....

   b. .... into ....

   c. .... into ....

   d. .... into ....

2. Look at the sample sentences in your dictionary for *convert* and its forms. What is being converted in each of those samples? What is it converted into?

   ....

   ....

   ....

3. Does *convert* have any forms that are not used in the sample sentences in the box above? If so, what are they? Consult your dictionary.

   ....

STEP II VOCABULARY ACTIVITIES: Sentence Level

Word Form Chart			
Noun	Verb	Adjective	Adverb
contradiction	contradict	contradictory contradicting	contradictorily*

C. Answer these questions in your notebook, using the forms of *contradict* in parentheses. Use each form of the word at least once. Refer to Reading 2 for information. Discuss your answers in a small group.

1. Why does the author of Reading 2 think it's unusual for young people to establish brands as a way of rebelling? (*contradictory* or *contradiction*)

2. Imagine a meeting of A-Ron and other culturally influential people from Lower Manhattan. How would these others react if A-Ron claims he is the top expert on the subculture there? (*contradict*)

3. Look again at the description of the store named "Supreme." Do you find anything strange about the store? What? (*contradictory* or *contradiction*)

4. The author writes, "They protest culture's materialism with their own style of materialism." Explain what this means. (*contradictory*)

D. Imagine that a financial institution is trying to find images that might help it build its brand. Which symbols would be most likely to register with potential clients? Rank them from *1* (most appealing) to *6* (least appealing).

.... a field of spring flowers in the sunshine

.... big buildings in a city center

.... a strong dog protecting a family

.... a large ship sailing calmly on rough waters

.... a fortress or castle

.... a young couple, smiling and relaxed

As a class, make a chart on the board and tally everyone's answers. Write a summary of the results using some of the target vocabulary from this unit. Include answers to these questions: Which symbol does your class think is the most effective for a bank to use? Least effective? Why?

---

*This form is rarely used. It is more common to see "in a contradictory way" or "in contradiction."

E. Look at these arguments for and against common branding practices. Restate each idea in your notebook, using some form of the word in parentheses. Then write a paragraph that expresses your own opinion. Try to use as many target words as possible. Be prepared to discuss your paragraph or debate the issue in class.

For	Against
People shouldn't think that branding is something new. Even in ancient Rome, businesses had slogans. (*presume*)	The use of branding in modern life is huge. The number of channels for advertising and image-building has multiplied many times since home computers became common. (*medium*)
People are eager to buy an image along with a product. Branding satisfies a need for belonging and self-definition. (*consume*)	For some people, brand images register too strongly. This keeps them from interacting honestly with other people. (*equate*)
Businesses operate in a crowded marketplace. They have to find a way to distinguish their products from competing products. (*corporate*)	Products should distinguish themselves by quality, value for money, or other traits that are really part of the product. Using brand images to entertain and distract people from these product-related qualities is dishonest. (*theme*)

F. Self-Assessment Review: Go back to page 15 and reassess your knowledge of the target vocabulary. How has your understanding of the words changed? What words do you feel most comfortable with now?

WRITING AND DISCUSSION TOPICS

1. Reading 2 mentions young people who express youthful rebellion by starting companies. Do you think Reading 2 really describes a new phenomenon or not? Explain your answer and use specific examples to support it.

2. The costs of branding are passed on to consumers. Companies pay for their ads and creative teams by raising prices or reducing services. Do you think this trade-off is good for consumers? Does the brand image associated with a product justify this extra expense?

3. Social-networking websites, like MySpace or Facebook, are supposed to be noncommercial. Users promise not to use the sites to promote products. In reality, though, users recommend their favorite bands, their favorite books, and so on. Brand developers have found ways to advertise without actually advertising. And they benefit from being attached to websites that feel comfortable and personal to their users. Do you think people who promote products should be banned from the websites for breaking the rules? Or is it unavoidable that advertising will leak onto these sites?

MACHINES THAT RECOGNIZE FACES

In this unit, you will

- ○ read about face-recognition technology and how its use affects societies.
- ○ learn to scan for important information in a text.
- ○ increase your understanding of the target academic words for this unit:

adjacent	consequent	device	involve	modify
analyze	controversy	equip	justify	monitor
anticipate	data	federal	legal	undertake

SELF-ASSESSMENT OF TARGET WORDS

Think carefully about how well you know each target word in this unit. Then, write it in the appropriate column in the chart.

I have never seen the word before.	I have seen the word but am not sure what it means.	I understand the word when I see or hear it in a sentence.	I have tried to use the word, but I am not sure I am using it correctly.	I use the word with confidence in either speaking *or* writing.	I use the word with confidence, both in speaking *and* writing.

MORE WORDS YOU'LL NEED

database: a set of information stored in a computer

threat: something that could cause harm

BEFORE YOU READ

Read these questions. Discuss your answers in a small group.

1. Imagine that someone has taken your picture without asking you. How would you feel? Explain why.

2. Police officers have difficulty spotting trouble in large crowds of people. How could technology help the police?

3. Have you ever seen a security camera? Where? Why do you think a camera was placed there?

READ

This article is about face-recognition technology used for security at sporting events. It focuses on the technology used at the 2001 Super Bowl—the championship American football game—held in Tampa, Florida.

Looking for Bad Guys at the Big Game

When the Super Bowl came to Tampa, Florida, in 2001, football players and coaches were not the only people on camera. Every fan was of interest to security officials, who used tiny, hard-
5 to-see cameras to capture a shot of each person who passed through the stadium gates.

The organizers of any huge sporting event have to **anticipate** trouble and try to stop it before it starts. Security officials at Tampa's
10 Raymond James Stadium hoped to do so by using machines that recognize faces. Each face seen by the gate-mounted cameras was compared to the **data** in local and **federal** law-enforcement computer systems. The data included photos of
15 people previously arrested for stealing, causing fights, and other **illegal** activities. A similar set of automatic eyes surveyed the crowds at The NFL Experience, a football-related exhibition **adjacent** to the stadium. If a fan's picture
20 matched one in the database, security officials could closely **monitor** him or her and perhaps even make an arrest.

Security cameras monitor fans at a sporting event.

Not everyone thinks this kind of surveillance is a good thing. It has stirred some **controversy**
25 about possible threats to the privacy rights of individuals. People being captured on camera were not told their pictures were being taken. None of them gave permission. The technology has not been proven to be reliable. What if
30 the system points out an innocent person as a criminal by mistake? At a very basic level, it simply makes many people angry to see elements of a "Big Brother" society, where authorities spy on people wherever they go, in the United States.

Security officials say the face-recognition (FR) system's great benefits **justify** any small inconvenience. Banks, shopping malls, and government buildings are already **equipped** with security cameras, and no one has a problem with that. Why complain about the system used at Raymond James Stadium?

One big difference is that a system like the one used at the Super Bowl **involves** "biometric" technology. It **analyzes** bodily characteristics (the features of the face) to establish a person's identity. A biometric system **undertakes** not just to display or record an event but to instantly identify the people involved in it.

The difference in types of systems is illustrated by another camera system in Tampa, this one in Ybor City, an entertainment district near downtown. At first, cameras mounted on the district's utility poles monitored the streets for fights, drug deals, and other crimes. The police might see a crime as it was happening or use the video to help in any **consequent** investigations.

Then Tampa **modified** those cameras to link directly to the police department's own database. This made them true biometric tools. Instead of humans analyzing a video to see who was depicted, machines did the identifying. Advocates of biometric systems say this makes the system more scientific. Computers can compare exact measurements of facial features in order to make matches. Opponents of such systems object. They argue that machines are easily fooled by such simple **devices** as hats, new hairstyles, or glasses. Humans are a lot better at recognizing individuals, they say, than computer systems are.

READING COMPREHENSION

Mark each sentence as *T* (true) or *F* (false) according to the information in Reading 1. Use the dictionary to help you understand new words.

.... **1.** Images of individuals tied to illegal activities were used in looking for criminal activity at the stadium.

.... **2.** Security officials felt that using face-recognition technology at the Super Bowl was a good idea.

.... **3.** Biometric technology analyzes part of a person's body to determine who he or she is.

.... **4.** All the photos in a face-recognition database come from the federal government.

.... **5.** A face-recognition system helps catch dangerous people who are still unknown to the police.

.... **6.** Face-matching systems have no trouble identifying someone wearing a hat or glasses.

READING STRATEGY: Scanning

Most readers remember only general information after reading a text. To find specific information, they go back and *scan* the reading. *Scanning* means quickly moving your eyes over the text to find specific things.

One method is to scan for *signals*:

- capital letters: for names of people, cities, countries, and special events
- numbers: for dates, measurements, statistics, and addresses
- symbols: for percentages, monetary amounts, email addresses, etc.
- **bold** or *italic* type: for words that receive special treatment or emphasis

Another method is to scan for *keywords*.

- specific words related to the information you want to find
- unusual letter groups that your eyes would more easily notice

Scan Reading 1 for specific information to answer these questions. Write the answer, the signal(s) or keyword(s) you scanned for, and the line numbers where you found each answer. Compare answers with a partner.

1. At which stadium was the Super Bowl played?

   Answer: *Raymond James Stadium*

   Character(s) or Keyword(s): *capital letters, stadium, Super Bowl*

   Lines: *10*

2. Where is Ybor City?

   Answer: ....

   Character(s) or Keyword(s): ....

   Lines: ....

3. When was the Super Bowl in Tampa, Florida?

   Answer: ....

   Character(s) or Keyword(s): ....

   Lines: ....

4. What is The NFL Experience?

   Answer: ....

   Character(s) or Keyword(s): ....

   Lines: ....

5. What is a "Big Brother" society?

   Answer: ....

   Character(s) or Keyword(s): ....

   Lines: ....

STEP I VOCABULARY ACTIVITIES: Word Level

A. Read these excerpts from another article on face-recognition technology. For each excerpt, cross out the one word or phrase in parentheses with a different meaning from the other three choices. Compare answers with a partner.

1. Some schools use a card-access security system. A student must insert a personal ID card into (*a device / a piece of equipment / some data / a machine*) in order to enter.

2. The problem is that people lose or forget their cards. A person (*involving / watching / monitoring / guarding*) the entrance will probably not recognize each student, especially at a big school.

3. (*Foreseeing / Anticipating / Predicting / Undertaking*) problems of this type, many schools have turned to video badging as a good backup for a card-access system.

4. With a video-badging system, images of every student are stored in a computer. A guard or monitor at a computer station (*inside / adjacent to / next to / near*) the entrance can type in the name of a student without a card and see the picture of that student.

5. Many corporate computer networks require employees to type in a password to identify themselves, but there are problems with this system, too. There are lots of ways to steal someone's password. (*Consequently / Therefore / As a result / Justifiably*), restricted information can be accessed by the wrong person.

6. But there's no practical way to steal someone's face. Facial recognition technology (*modifies / analyzes / examines / inspects*) facial features much like a handwriting expert would look at someone's signature.

The word *modify* is similar in meaning to the word *change*. It means "to change something slightly," usually in order to improve it.

The word *device* refers to a tool, machine, or system made for a specific purpose. For example, a knife is a device for cutting things.

B. Put a check (✓) next to the items that would be helpful devices for a police officer. In a small group, discuss why you made your choices. Then, discuss how each device could be modified for use by people in their homes.

.... 1. an infrared camera   .... 5. a high-power flashlight

.... 2. fingerprint powder   .... 6. plastic straps that lock in place

.... 3. a walkie-talkie   .... 7. an electronic navigation system

.... 4. a lie detector   .... 8. a bicycle

STEP II VOCABULARY ACTIVITIES: Sentence Level

Word Form Chart for *involve*			
Noun	Verb	Adjective	Adverb
involvement	involve	involved	....

The word *involve* has the core meaning of "include" or "connect." The passive verb form usually takes the preposition *in*.

Mark was **involved in** security efforts at the game.

Her work **involved** testing security systems.

The **involvement** of local police helped reduce crime in the neighborhood.

As an adjective, *involved* has the same meaning as "complicated." It is often used with the word *long* to describe a series of tasks or an event with many parts to it, such as "a long, involved process" or "a long, involved ceremony."

C. Answer the questions using the form of *involve* in parentheses. Refer to Reading 1 for information. Compare answers with a partner.

1. How did they use face-recognition technology at The NFL Experience? (*involved*)

   ....

2. Why might a person's photo be in the database of a face-recognition system? (*involvement*)

   ....

3. What places typically use security cameras? (*involved*)

   ....

4. Why is face-recognition technology called "biometric"? (*involve*)

   ....

5. How did Tampa modify the security system in Ybor City? (*involve*)

   ....

Word Form Chart

Noun	Verb	Adjective	Adverb
anticipation	anticipate	anticipatory	....
consequence consequences	....	consequent	consequently
controversy	....	controversial	controversially
justification	justify	justifiable justified justifying unjustified	justifiably
modification	modify	modified modifying unmodified	....

D. Read these excerpts from another article about face-recognition technology. Then, in your notebook, restate each excerpt using the words in parentheses. Do not change the meanings of the sentences. Be prepared to read aloud or discuss your sentences in class.

1. Critics of face-recognition (FR) technology have good reasons to question its accuracy. (*justifiably*)

2. According to one study, the very best FR systems are only about one-third as accurate as human beings. Such findings have fueled a debate within the security industry: Are FR systems a waste of money? (*consequence* or *consequently, controversy*)

3. Developers of FR software cannot know in advance how a face might change from one photo to the next. (*anticipate*)

4. The software is constantly being improved, but image changes caused by aging, lighting, or camera angle still confuse it. (*modify* or *modification*)

5. A human's brain, however, has been practicing recognizing faces since birth. As a result, most people can see past even large changes in another's appearance. (*consequence*)

6. Does it make sense to spend billions of dollars to create automatic FR systems when top-quality "systems" are all around us? (*justified* or *justifiable*)

7. When technicians look ahead to all the possible problems in a human-centered system, most say that it does make sense to create FR systems. (*anticipate* or *anticipation*)

8. A person may be very reliable when full of energy and fully focused on an FR task. But humans do not stay that way for very long. They get tired, stressed out, bored, hungry, sick, distracted, and even angry. All these conditions can greatly affect their reliability. (*consequences*)

9. Although automatic FR systems will always have their opponents, it makes sense to keep improving them and using them. They are a better option than a room full of tired people. (*controversial, modifications*)

BEFORE YOU READ

Read these questions. Discuss your answers in a small group.

1. Have you ever needed to prove your identity? If so, when? How did you prove it?

2. You probably have at least one picture ID (an identification document with your photograph). It may be a passport, a school ID card, or a driver's license. Do you think the picture looks like you? Why or why not? Do you think the picture could look like someone else?

3. Why might someone try to hide his or her true identity? What techniques would such a person use? Is it always wrong to pretend that you are someone else? Why or why not?

READ

This reading examines the usefulness of face-recognition technology for airport security.

A Face in the Airport Crowd

Security cameras at the airport in Portland, Maine, scanned travelers as usual on the morning of September 11, 2001. Just before 6:00 A.M., two young men with tickets to Boston passed
5   a camera adjacent to their gate. Within a few hours, they would board American Airlines flight 11 out of Boston, hijack[1] it, and fly it into New York's World Trade Center.

The security video was shown on television
10 nine days later. A controversy arose. Why hadn't the Federal Bureau of Investigation (FBI) stopped those men? The cameras had caught them. Why couldn't the FBI, or security guards, or someone else see that those men were
15 dangerous?

Such questions are justifiable, but not very realistic. The terrorists were not doing anything unusual on the video. From their appearance, no one could anticipate their future criminal
20 activity. Unless someone at the airport already knew who they were and what they were planning, there would be no reason to stop

them. But the security video did inspire some thinking about new possibilities. What if a
25 machine "knew" what millions of bad guys looked like and could recognize them when they tried to board airplanes?

This idea called for modifying an old idea, face-recognition (FR) technology, for a new
30 purpose—airport security. In an FR system, a computer holds a large gallery of photos taken at some earlier time. As someone walks past the system's camera, his or her face is matched against the stored photos. If the computer sees a
35 match, it sends out an alarm.

Boston's Logan Airport undertook the first test of an airport FR system in 2002. Because more than half of the September 11 hijackers had flown out of Logan, a working FR system
40 there would have special meaning. Logan's test system was very small. Still, it provided an interesting look at how well the technology might work.

The test involved 40 airport workers,
45 whose photographs were put into the system's database. These workers then blended in with

[1] *hijack*: take by force, usually an airplane or other form of transport

the airport crowd. They filed past digital security cameras like everyone else. If the system was working correctly, it would send out a warning when any of the 40 workers appeared on camera (a positive match). It should *not* send out warnings about other people in the airport. Such a mistaken result, called a false positive, could have serious consequences, including expensive lawsuits.

After about three months, the test system was evaluated. It had not worked well at all. More than one-third of the time, it had failed to recognize one of the 40 airport workers (a "false acceptance"). More than half of the warnings it did send out were false positives.

Security officers who monitored the FR system during the test had an exhausting experience. Because the system made so many mistakes, they had to work frantically to double-check all the matches. Under all this stress, the officers made frequent mistakes themselves. All in all, the system just made more work for humans.

The exact reasons for such poor performance are unclear, but analysts can make some good guesses. The National Institute for Standards and Technology (NIST), a federal government agency, occasionally tests FR programs. In a 2002 trial, it evaluated ten systems, each made by a different company. Some important data came from the NIST study:

- The best system, working indoors with new database photos, can be about 90 percent successful.

- That same system, if moved outdoors, becomes highly unreliable. A system that is 94% effective indoors is only about 54% effective outdoors.

- Old database photos are difficult to match. The reliability of an FR system decreases by about 5% each year as the database photo gets older. In other words, if a system had a

75% chance of matching an image with a new database photo, it would have only a 70% chance of matching with a one-year-old photo, 65% with a two-year-old photo, and so on.

- Differences in camera angle cause a lot of trouble in an FR system.

- As databases of stored photos get larger, FR systems get less dependable. Each time the size of a database doubles, the system's reliability goes down by 2 to 3 percentage points.

In the test at Logan Airport, lighting was probably not the problem. All the cameras were indoors. The size and quality of the database were probably not to blame either. It contained only 40 photos, all of them recent.

Almost certainly, the images from security equipment looked too different from database photos. Camera angle was probably a big factor.

None of the 40 airport workers in the test wore any disguises. If someone had worn one of the classic devices—a fake beard, dummy glasses, a false nose or chin—the FR system could probably not make a match. Even minor, everyday changes in appearance seem to have confused the system. A new hairstyle, different makeup, an unusual facial expression, or a tilt of the head could be enough to make the computer believe there is no match.

The bottom line is that an automatic FR system cannot dependably pick a terrorist out of an airport crowd. For one thing, any real-life database is unlikely to contain photos of many potential terrorists. Most of them have not yet done anything illegal, so they are unknown to law enforcement before they strike. For another, computer software is too inflexible to adjust to many of the changes that occur in the real world. With current technology, no FR system can even approach the human mind's ability to compare images and decide whether they match.

READING COMPREHENSION

Mark each sentence as *T* (true) or *F* (false) according to the information in Reading 2. Use the dictionary to help you understand new words.

.... **1.** Security cameras at the Portland airport caught images of the two terrorists who passed them.

.... **2.** It is good for a face-recognition system to make a positive match.

.... **3.** It is good for a face-recognition system to make a false positive.

.... **4.** The system tested at Logan Airport made work easier for security officers.

.... **5.** A face-recognition system using recent database photos is probably more accurate than one using old photos.

.... **6.** The reliability of a system improves as the size of its database increases.

.... **7.** Disguises such as false beards or fake noses can cause a system to make mistakes.

.... **8.** Humans are better at face-recognition than computer-based systems are.

READING STRATEGY

Complete the chart by scanning Reading 2 for the answer to each question. Fill in the missing information.

Question	Answer	Signals and Keywords	Lines
1. What is the full name of the FBI?	The Federal Bureau of Investigation	capital letters	11
2. Where is Logan Airport?			
3. How many airport workers were pictured in the test database?			
4. What is the NIST?			
5. What is a false positive?			
6. If a system is 94% effective indoors, how effective will it be outdoors?			
7. How much does a system's reliability decrease each year as a database photo gets older?			

STEP I VOCABULARY ACTIVITIES: Word Level

A. Complete the sentences about writer Philip K. Dick by using words from the target vocabulary list. Use each item one time. The synonyms in parentheses can help you.

> adjacent   devices   monitor
> analyzes   involved in   undertook
> anticipate   involving

.... **a.** The science-fiction author Philip K. Dick, or PKD, had an amazing ability to .... the effects of future technology on society.
(see in advance)

.... **b.** Berkeley in the 1950s and 1960s was a center for radical thought and unusual lifestyles. PKD was .... the area's "beat" poet culture.
(part of)

.... **c.** Technological .... such as face-recognition systems and eye scanners play a special role in PKD's stories.
(tools)

.... **d.** He was born in Chicago, Illinois, but he lived most of his life in California. He went to high school in Berkeley, a city .... to San Francisco.
(next to)

.... **e.** In 1974, he began to have disturbing visions, some .... dreams of himself as a first-century Roman citizen who was trying to hide from government authorities.
(including)

.... **f.** In 1982, the now-classic movie *Blade Runner* was released. It was based on his story *Do Androids Dream of Electric Sheep?* Like all of Dick's best work, it .... human identity in a world of powerful machines.
(examines)

.... **g.** PKD started college in Berkeley, but he dropped out. He worked at a record store until he sold his first short story in 1952. At that point, he .... fiction writing as a full-time job.
(tried to succeed at)

.... **h.** These visions shaped his thinking and writing. In some of his books, the main character struggles to break free from technology that helps the government .... all human action and thought.
(watch over)

B. Tell the story of Philip K. Dick's life by putting the sentences in activity A into a logical order. Number them from *1* to *8* (more than one sequence may be possible). Then, use the target words as you compare stories with a partner.

C. Read these sample sentences that feature the forms of *analyze*. Then answer the questions that follow, using a dictionary as suggested. Compare answers with a partner.

> **a.** After we collected information, we had to *analyze* it.
> **b.** According to government *analysts*, the traffic problem can be solved only by building a new road.
> **c.** An *analysis* of the neighborhood's water showed several harmful chemicals.
> **d.** After *analyzing* its purchasing system, the company decided to make some changes.

1. Put a check (✓) next to the word closest in meaning to *analyze*. Consult your dictionary before you answer.

   .... judge .... combine .... examine .... understand

2. Each of these sentences indicates that something was analyzed. What was analyzed?

   a. ....

   b. ....

   c. ....

   d. ....

3. Look at the sample sentences in your dictionary for *analyze* and its forms. What is being analyzed in each of those samples?

4. Does *analyze* have any forms that are not used in the sample sentences in the box above? If so, what are they? Consult your dictionary.

STEP II VOCABULARY ACTIVITIES: Sentence Level

D. In a small group, discuss these questions. Use a dictionary to clarify word meanings if needed.

1. Who should make airports secure?

   a. the federal government   **c.** the local police

   b. airlines   **d.** travelers

2. Think about a culture you know well. Which of these activities do law enforcement officers monitor? Why?

   a. public gatherings on a holiday   **c.** sporting events

   b. teachers talking to their students   **d.** buying and selling at shops

3. What might be some consequences of each of these situations? Which consequences are good and which are bad?

   a. losing your ID card

   b. using a security system before it is tested

   c. putting security cameras in a store

   d. using a database of old photos in an FR system

Privacy allows you to live your life without unwanted attention from others. Your privacy is violated when someone—a neighbor, a salesperson, an email spammer, or the government—learns too much about you or what you are doing. Opponents of automated FR and other security technology say it threatens personal privacy. Supporters of the technology say that some violations of privacy are necessary to make society safe. The controversy is about priorities: Is public security more important than personal privacy?

E. In each of these situations, there has been some loss of personal privacy. Write *Y* in the blank when you think the loss of privacy is justified. Write *N* when you think the loss of privacy is not justified. In your notebook, write a short explanation for each of your answers. Be prepared to read aloud or discuss your opinions in class.

.... 1. The police set up cameras to watch people throughout the city.

.... 2. Security cameras at a sporting event take pictures of everyone who enters the stadium.

.... 3. A school takes a picture of each of its students.

.... 4. A school sells pictures of its students to an advertising agency looking for models.

.... 5. Pictures of criminals are loaded into a database.

.... 6. Pictures of everyone who has a driver's license are loaded into a database.

.... 7. Cameras in an airport take pictures of the crowd.

.... 8. Cameras at a movie theater take pictures of the crowd.

F. Look at these arguments for and against the use of face-recognition technology in public places. Restate each idea in your notebook, using the word in parentheses. Then write a paragraph that expresses your own opinion. Try to use as many target words as possible in your work. Be prepared to present your work or debate the issue in class.

For	Against
The security of the public is more important than the privacy of the individual. Some loss of privacy is necessary to keep people safe. (*justified*)	The government should protect all individual rights, including the right to privacy. Citizens should not have to give up their rights in order to be safe. (*justified*)
Small weaknesses in security can lead to horrible things. Think of September 11. A little more watchfulness could have saved thousands of lives. (*consequences*)	The horrible events of September 11 should not distract us from our ideals. The worst possible effect of such terrorism would be the loss of our basic freedoms. (*consequences*)
Technology can be powerful enough to catch the bad guys without affecting innocent people. We should keep improving face-recognition systems to fulfill their potential. (*undertake* and *devices*)	Face-recognition systems will always make a lot of mistakes. It would be a waste of time to try making a system sensitive enough to all the changes that can occur in a person's appearance. (*undertake* and *devices*)

G. Self-Assessment Review: Go back to page 29 and reassess your knowledge of the target vocabulary. How has your understanding of the words changed? What words do you feel most comfortable with now?

WRITING AND DISCUSSION TOPICS

1. Privacy experts are worried that face-recognition technology will enable the government to monitor the lives of people unnecessarily. Do you share this concern or not? Explain your answer by referring to specific aspects of the average person's life (sleeping, meeting with friends, emailing, etc.).

2. Research by the National Institute of Standards and Technology (NIST) has shown that a person's age and gender affect the accuracy of face-recognition technology. Males are easier for a system to recognize than females are. Older people are easier than younger people. Why might this be true?

3. Imagine a face-recognition database that includes a picture of everyone with a driver's license or a passport. Consider the advantages and disadvantages. Whose pictures would you include in a "perfect" database?

4. Some people claim that the best biometric system is genetic. They point out that police and the courts use DNA to make extremely accurate identifications. ID cards with a person's genetic information may someday be created. Do you think such a system would be good or bad? What benefits do you anticipate? What problems?

HOW COULD THEY DO THAT?

In this unit, you will

- ➲ read about two remarkable figures in English literature—William Shakespeare and Joseph Conrad.
- ➲ learn to make a simple outline of a text.
- ➲ increase your understanding of the target academic words for this unit:

accumulate	debate	invest	protocol	text
adequate	depress	persist	reluctance	volume
author	indicate	precede	sustain	

SELF-ASSESSMENT OF TARGET WORDS

Think carefully about how well you know each target word in this unit. Then, write it in the appropriate column in the chart.

I have never seen the word before.	I have seen the word but am not sure what it means.	I understand the word when I see or hear it in a sentence.	I have tried to use the word, but I am not sure I am using it correctly.	I use the word with confidence in either speaking *or* writing.	I use the word with confidence, both in speaking *and* writing.

MORE WORDS YOU'LL NEED

hoax: a trick that is played on somebody

multilingual: able to use more than one language

noble: belonging to a high social class in a country with a king or queen

BEFORE YOU READ

Read these questions. Discuss your answers in a small group.

1. Who was William Shakespeare? Why is he famous?

2. Have you ever seen or read a famous play? Briefly describe it.

3. How would you feel if you found out that a book by your favorite writer was actually written by someone else? Would it matter to you? Why or why not?

READ

Read this article describing two points of view about the authorship of William Shakespeare's plays.

Could Shakespeare Have Written Shakespeare's Plays?

William Shakespeare

Edward de Vere

Literary detectives have uncovered many facts about William Shakespeare. Still, the most important question of all remains: Did he really write the Shakespeare plays? Sir
5 Francis Bacon, Christopher Marlowe, the Earl of Southampton (Shakespeare's patron), and even Queen Elizabeth herself have at times been suspected of writing them. The sheer **volume** of Shakespeare's work—37 plays, 154
10 sonnets, 2 other poems, and an elegy—has led to suggestions that "William Shakespeare" was actually several people, not one.

The strongest current **debate** is between groups known as the Oxfordians and the
15 Stratfordians. Oxfordians say that Edward de Vere, the 17th Earl of Oxford, wrote the plays under the pen name[1] William Shakespeare. Stratfordians say that the works were all written by William Shakespeare, an actor known to have
20 been born at Stratford in 1564. The challenge for both sides is to produce solid evidence. So far, neither side has come up with much.

Oxfordians say the actor Shakespeare was too poorly educated to have been the **author** of
25 the plays. He was the son of a tradesman, and there is no record that he had any schooling. There is no evidence that he ever traveled outside southern England. He was just an actor and an occasional real-estate **investor**. His will
30 mentions no writings, and there is no evidence he ever owned a book. A background like that could not have been **adequate** for writing such brilliant plays. The life of Edward de Vere, on the other hand, was more than adequate. His
35 education was the best money could buy. He was intimately familiar with England's noble families. He traveled to many of the locations important in Shakespeare's plays, including France, Scotland, and Italy.
40 The de Vere theory gained a lot of support after 1991. In that year, researchers began studying the handwritten notes in de Vere's

---

[1] *pen name*: the name a writer chooses to use when publishing his or her work

copy of a 1569 edition of the Bible. About 1000 Bible passages are underlined or otherwise
45 marked. Nearly 25 percent of them match up with parts of Shakespeare's work. Probably not a coincidence, say the Oxfordians. For example, part of Act V in *The Merchant of Venice* speaks of a good deed shining out "in a naughty world." One
50 of the passages de Vere underlined in his Bible contains the phrase, "a naughty and crooked nation, among whom ye shine as lights in the world."

Stratfordians reply, "Why look beyond
55 William Shakespeare of Stratford?" He was not the backward son of a lowly family, as many claim. His father was a prosperous merchant who held the town's highest office (high bailiff). The King's New School in Stratford offered an
60 excellent education. Although school records cannot be found, it is likely that the town's high bailiff sent his son there. Shakespeare moved to London in the late 1580s, in his early twenties. There he became famous and wealthy as an actor
65 and as London's leading playwright. And certain aspects of his life seem to match better with the plays than de Vere's do. For example, the perceptive portrayal of emotional **depression** in *Hamlet* seems to **indicate** that the author had
70 experienced the ailment. *Hamlet* was written around the year 1600, four years after William Shakespeare's only son, Hamnet, died at the age of 11.

Stratfordians also point out that the de Vere
75 theory assumes an unlikely hoax. The Oxford camp claims that de Vere wanted to hide his authorship because it went against **protocol** for the noble class. A highborn earl simply should not be writing plays for common people. To give
80 de Vere cover, William Shakespeare of Stratford

must have agreed (probably for pay) to serve as a front man[2]. The Stratfordians point out that, for this to be true, Shakespeare's many friends and acquaintances were either blind enough
85 to be fooled by it or willing to be in on the trick. The same goes for de Vere's friends and acquaintances, including the very intelligent Queen Elizabeth. The part hardest to believe is that a scheme like that could be **sustained** for
90 decades without the secret being revealed.

Another difficulty for the Oxfordians is that the 17th Earl of Oxford died in 1604. Many of the greatest plays were produced after this date. *Macbeth*, for example, dates from 1606–1607
95 and *The Tempest* from 1611. A great deal of careful work has confirmed these dates, and most Oxfordians reluctantly concede that de Vere's death **preceded** the appearance of these plays. But the Oxford camp **persists** in maintaining
100 their position. They argue that de Vere wrote them before he died and that they were brought out as needed for performance. Also, the **texts** of many Shakespeare plays contain references to events after 1604. The Oxfordians say someone
105 must have added contemporary references to make the plays look timely.

Any debate centered on speculation alone will probably last a very long time. Neither side in this debate seems likely to **accumulate**
110 the evidence necessary to be able to settle the matter. As one researcher, Al Austin, summarizes the controversy, "Those who believe de Vere was Shakespeare must accept an improbable hoax as part of it, a conspiracy of silence involving
115 among others, Queen Elizabeth herself. Those who side with the Stratford man must believe in miracles."

---

[2] *front man*: a person who agrees to pretend to be someone else in the eyes of the public

READING COMPREHENSION

Mark each sentence as *T* (true) or *F* (false) according to the information in Reading 1. Use the dictionary to help you understand new words.

.... **1.** There is serious debate about whether Shakespeare's plays were really written by Edward de Vere.

.... **2.** Unlike Shakespeare, de Vere is known to have traveled to locations important in the plays.

.... **3.** Stratfordians say that even though Shakespeare was uneducated, he taught himself enough to have written the plays.

.... **4.** About one-quarter of the Bible passages that de Vere highlighted are very similar to passages in Shakespearean plays.

.... **5.** Oxfordians say that Shakespeare agreed to pretend that he wrote the plays, even though de Vere really wrote them.

.... **6.** Many Shakespearean plays first appeared after de Vere's death.

.... **7.** Stratfordians say it's unlikely de Vere could have hidden his authorship from so many people for so long.

.... **8.** New evidence is likely to settle the Oxford–Stratford debate within the next few years.

READING STRATEGY: Outlining

One way to better understand a reading is to outline it. Outlining helps you see how the text is organized so that you can figure out the main ideas and details.

In a common outlining system, Roman numerals (I, II, III, etc.) show the major ideas or sections in a reading. The next level of detail is indicated with capital letters.

The outlining system becomes more involved as the complexity of a text increases. For more information on outlining, go online and do a search for "how to outline".

Complete the outline of Reading 1 with phrases from the box.

Details of the Oxford position
Evidence from the 1556 Bible
Shakespeare's likely attendance at a good school
Matching Shakespeare's plays with his life

The problem of de Vere's 1604 death
Shakespeare's weak background
Stratfordian position

Could Shakespeare Have Written Shakespeare's Plays?

I. Introduction

II. General description of the Oxford–Stratford debate
   A. Oxfordian position
   B. ....

III. *Details of the Oxfordian position* ....
   A. ....
   B. de Vere's strong background
   C. ....

IV. Details of the Stratfordian position
   A. Prominence of Shakespeare's family
   B. ....
   C. Shakespeare's prosperity and importance in London
   D. ....
   E. An unlikely hoax necessary for Oxfordian position

V. ....
   A. Dates of plays after 1604
   B. Oxfordian explanations

VI. Likely future of the debate

STEP 1 VOCABULARY ACTIVITIES: Word Level

A. Read these excerpts from another article about Shakespeare's work. For each excerpt, cross out the one word or phrase in parentheses with a different meaning from the other three choices. Compare answers with a partner.

1. None of Shakespeare's plays has survived in the form of a manuscript in the (*author's / sculptor's / writer's / playwright's*) own handwriting. Consequently, we do not know for certain which words Shakespeare actually wrote.

2. Unfortunately, printing companies at the time were not very reliable. Errors usually (*built up / accumulated / occurred / multiplied*) in a work during the stages of preparation for printing.

3. Errors were also introduced by the people who set the type. They might change what a manuscript said just because their supply of letters was not (*relevant / sufficient / enough / adequate*) to spell what the author wrote.

4. We have no way of knowing how to fix the errors. For example, the earliest printed (*texts / copies / protocols / versions*) of *King Lear* and *Richard III* are obviously incorrect, but we have no way of knowing how to restore them to Shakespeare's original versions.

The word *precede* means "come before" or "happen earlier than." The first step in a process precedes the second step. The second step precedes the third. Viewed another way, the second step *follows* the first.

B. Put a check (✓) next to the statements that correctly describe the order of events in Reading 1. Rewrite the unchecked sentences and correct the order. Discuss your answers with a partner.

.... **1.** The writing of *Hamlet* preceded the writing of *Macbeth*.

.... **2.** De Vere's death preceded Shakespeare's.

.... **3.** Shakespeare's move to London followed his rise to fame.

.... **4.** The publication of de Vere's Bible preceded Shakespeare's birth.

.... **5.** The publication of *Hamlet* followed the death of Shakespeare's son.

.... **6.** De Vere's death followed the production of *The Tempest*.

The word *protocol* refers to the system of rules for correct behavior. It is often used in formal, official contexts. People can *follow protocol*, *go against protocol*, or *break protocol*.

> Many say he broke **protocol** when he preceded the president into the room.

Note: Today, *protocol* also refers to the set of signals and rules that control how information is sent from one computer to another. For example, the abbreviation *http* at the beginning of many website addresses stands for "hypertext transfer protocol."

C. Match each type of protocol with the example of it. Compare answers with a partner. Then, write an example of your own for each type of protocol in your notebook.

.... **1.** military protocol

a. Type the words in the SEARCH field and put quotation marks around them in order to get the most relevant hits.

.... **2.** social protocol

b. All managers must explain company email policies to new employees on their first day of work.

.... **3.** research protocol

c. Never turn your back on an officer without first saluting and having that salute returned.

.... **4.** business protocol

d. Speaker A has two minutes. Then Speaker B has one minute to address Speaker A's points.

.... **5.** medical protocol

e. To the bride, you say, "Good luck." To the groom, you say, "Congratulations."

.... **6.** meeting protocol

f. Take one pill every six hours for four days, then reduce the dosage to one pill every twelve hours for two days.

STEP II VOCABULARY ACTIVITIES: Sentence Level

Word Form Chart

Noun	Verb	Adjective	Adverb
accumulation	accumulate	accumulated	....
author	author	authorial	authorially
debate	debate	debatable	debatably
sustenance sustainability	sustain	sustainable sustained	sustainably
volume	....	voluminous	voluminously

D. Read another story about Shakespeare's works. Then, in your notebook, restate the sentences, using the words in parentheses. Be prepared to read aloud or discuss your work in class.

1. When William Shakespeare died, he left a small amount of money in his will to actors John Hemminge and Henry Condell. (*author*)

2. Within seven years of Shakespeare's death in 1616, they had arranged 36 of Shakespeare's plays into one of the landmark publications in English letters—a collection now known as the *First Folio*. (*voluminous*)

3. Several unauthorized versions of each play, called foul copies, were in circulation. No one could say for sure how these compared to what Shakespeare intended. (*debatable*)

4. Since Hemminge and Condell had enjoyed a long-term working relationship with Shakespeare, they were in a good position to separate good versions from bad ones. (*sustained*)

5. Still, they had not worked on every play with Shakespeare. Some foul copies were probably close to accurate, but how could they tell? Errors tended to give birth to other errors. (*accumulation*)

6. Hemminge and Condell did their best, and 1623 marked the release of 700 copies of the 900-page *Mr. William Shakespeares Comedies, Histories & Tragedies. Published according to the True Originall Copies.* (*volume*)

E. Read the story in activity D again. Imagine you are a journalist who is interviewing the ghost of William Shakespeare about the *First Folio* and other editions of his plays. Prepare interview questions, using the cues provided, and write them in your notebook. Be prepared to act out your interview with a partner.

1. what / text

   What is your opinion of the texts included in the First Folio?

2. how / invest

3. how / sustain

4. who / adequate

5. who / author

Word Form Chart			
Noun	Verb	Adjective	Adverb
indication indicator	indicate	indicative indicated	....

F. Write the answers to the questions in your notebook, using the form of _indicate_ in parentheses. Refer to Reading 1 for information. Compare sentences with a partner.

1. Why do most scholars agree that whoever wrote the Shakespeare plays must have had a good education? (_indicative_)

2. What is the significance of Shakespeare's father having been the high bailiff of Stratford? (_indicate_)

3. Why are the highlighted passages in Edward de Vere's Bible important? (_indication_)

4. What is the relationship between the lack of solid evidence and the probable length of the debate ? (_indicator_)

READING 2

BEFORE YOU READ

Read these questions. Discuss your answers in a small group.

1. How many languages can you speak or write? Are you more comfortable speaking them or writing them?

2. What is the best way for you to expand your vocabulary in a second or third language? Reading? Listening? Real-world interactions? Observing others?

READ

This reading examines some possible reasons for Joseph Conrad's exceptional ability to write in English, which he learned only as an adult.

Fame in a Foreign Language: Joseph Conrad

Literary success is hard enough to achieve in one's native language. Very few authors cansustain themselves on money earned through writing. For a nonnative speaker of a language,
5 literary success in that language is extremely rare. Yet the English-language novels of Joseph Conrad indicate that it is not impossible.

Conrad was born Jozef Teodor Konrad Korzeniowski in 1857, in an area of present-day
10 Ukraine that was then a part of Poland. He was born into a noble family that owned a good deal of land and had its own crest. Russia ruled Poland at the time, and both of Conrad's parents took part in the struggle for independence.
15 Conrad's father was arrested in 1861 for revolutionary activity, and the family was exiled to the remote city of Vologda, in northern

Russia. The long winters and difficult living conditions there were too much for Conrad's mother. She died of tuberculosis when Conrad was only seven years old. His father's health suffered, too. The Russian government finally allowed the father and son to return to Poland, to the city of Krakow, but the father soon died. Conrad was eleven at the time.

His early life with his parents almost certainly influenced his success with languages. His father was clearly good at them—skillful enough to translate written texts into Polish from French and English. Like many well-born Poles at the time, Conrad learned French early in life. Given Russia's domination of Poland and his family's exile in Russia, Conrad must have learned some Russian as well.

He lived with his grandmother after his father's death. He did not invest much energy in his schoolwork, including his required classes in Latin and German. Restless and unhappy, he declared at the age of 14 that he wanted to be a

Joseph Conrad

sailor. In 1874, at the age of 16, Conrad traveled to France to learn commercial sailing and to avoid being drafted into the Russian army. His French language skills were more than adequate for his duties during the four years he spent in the French merchant marine. His career was interrupted by a suicide attempt, perhaps brought on by worry over debts from wild living in the south of France. Conrad recovered, but if he stayed in France the government would probably turn him over to the Russians for military service. He had to leave, so he went to England.

He signed on at the age of 20 as a seaman on an English steamer, but he did not need to speak very much English to get by. Ordinary seamen on vessels like his spoke many different languages and developed their own mixed language to communicate. However, protocol in the British merchant marine required ambitious sailors to pass through several levels before commanding a vessel. Each level had its own test, in English. By reading in English as much as he could, he became good enough to pass the written tests for second-class seaman, then first-class, then master. He sailed under the flag of Britain for a total of 16 years, and he became a British subject in 1886.

Throughout his life, Conrad was more inclined to read and write than to speak. He was often depressed and socially uncomfortable. This was probably one reason why, despite his phenomenal skills in English writing, he was very reluctant to speak English. A strong Polish accent persisted throughout his life. Even his wife and children said it made him hard to understand. French remained the language he was most comfortable speaking for the rest of his life.

By the time his first novel, *Almayer's Folly*, was published in 1895, there was no doubt that English was the language in which he would write. He had accumulated an immense vocabulary. His style was intriguing but not foreign-sounding. In fact, he wrote with a directness and plain style that were about 30 years ahead of their time. Some of his works, especially *Heart of Darkness* (1902) and *Nostromo* (1904), still sound reasonably modern.

Why Conrad became such a master of written English will always be a matter of debate. He himself wrote that the rhythms of the language

matched some inner sense that had been with him since birth. As he once wrote, "If I had not written in English, I would not have written at all." He never wrote professionally in either of
95 the languages that preceded English in his life, Polish and French.

Psychologists have guessed that Conrad associated these other languages with unpleasant experiences—his exile, his parents'
100 deaths, his attempted suicide. Also, the experiences that shaped Conrad's earliest novels were lived in English. English might have been established in Conrad's mind as the language of adult experience. These guesses make a lot of
105 sense. A large volume of research indicates that multilingual people tend to link some aspects of life with one language and other aspects with another.

By the time he died in 1924, at the age of 67,
110 Conrad had a secure place in 20th-century English literature. He was a personal friend of such greats as H.G. Wells and Ford Madox Ford. Some critics sniped at him for not being "really English," for using French-based vocabulary
115 instead of Anglo-Saxon stock (e.g. *arrest* instead of *stop*), or for letting some Polish influences show through his English. Almost no one now remembers who these critics were.

READING STRATEGY

Complete this outline of Reading 2 with your own words.

   I. Introduction

  II. ....

       A. Birth in Poland

       B. Exile to Russia

       C. Death of parents

 III. ....

  IV. Conrad's teen years

       A. ....

       B. ....

       C. ....

    V. ....

       A. Lack of need for English as a seaman

       B. ....

       C. Length of service

  VI. Conrad's spoken English

 VII. ....

VIII. Explanations for Conrad's literary ability in English

       A. ....

       B. ....

  IX. Conrad's position in English literature

READING COMPREHENSION

Mark each sentence as *T* (true) or *F* (false) according to the information in Reading 2. Use the dictionary to help you understand new words.

.... **1.** Joseph Conrad spoke two other languages before he learned English.

.... **2.** Conrad didn't invest much energy in school, preferring to go to sea instead.

.... **3.** Sailing protocol demanded that any sailor working on a British ship had to pass a large volume of tests in English.

.... **4.** Conrad felt that English had a rhythm that matched some inner feeling he had.

.... **5.** Most of his novels had to be translated into English from French or Polish.

.... **6.** Conrad spoke French, but only reluctantly and not well.

.... **7.** Conrad may have written in English because he associated the language with experiences in his adult life.

STEP I VOCABULARY ACTIVITIES: Word Level

A. Complete the sentences about synaesthesia by using words from the target vocabulary list. Use each item one time. The synonyms in parentheses can help you.

adequate	debate	persisted	reluctant
authors	indicates	precedes	

1. Joseph Conrad and Vladimir Nabokov, two famous .... , each
   (writers)
   had a form of synaesthesia—a condition in which two or more senses, such as
   hearing and sight, work together.

2. The most common form of synaesthesia involves a link between music and colors.
   The sound of a musical note .... the visual perception of color.
   (comes earlier than)

3. Conrad said that he preferred to write in English because it matched an inner
   sense of rhythm that had .... ever since his childhood.
   (continued)

4. Nabokov's autobiography, *Speak, Memory*, ... that he perceived
   (shows)
   letters as colors. For example, the sound of the letter "i" was white and the letter
   "c" was light blue.

5. Among researchers, there is much .... about whether the brain
   (argument)
   activity that happens during synaesthesia is related to language ability.

6. Most scientists are .... to claim a clear connection between
   (unwilling)
   synaesthesia and language because they lack .... experimental
   (enough)
   evidence.

B. Many academic words are also considered formal words. Which of the target words in this unit (see the chart on page 43) are more formal synonyms for these informal words? Be sure to use the right form of the target words.

Informal	Formal
1. continue	....
2. deep sadness	....
3. enough	....
4. show	....
5. amount	....
6. writer	....

C. Read these sample sentences that feature forms of _precede_. Then answer the questions that follow, using a dictionary as suggested. Compare answers with a partner.

> **a.** In the life cycle of a butterfly, the larva stage _precedes_ the pupa stage.
> **b.** If we let one person skip the test, it will set a bad _precedent_, and everyone will ask to skip it.
> **c.** Crops failed that year because, in _preceding_ years, very little rain had fallen.
> **d.** In a well-run university, the best interests of the students take _precedence_ over all other concerns.

1. Put a check (✓) next to the word closest in meaning to _precede_. Consult a dictionary before you answer.

   .... supersede   .... predate   .... validate   .... forestall

2. Look at the sample sentences in your dictionary for _precede_ and its forms. In each of those samples, what is coming before something else?

3. Does _precede_ have any forms that are not used in the sample sentences in the box above? If so, what are they? Consult your dictionary.

   ....

STEP II VOCABULARY ACTIVITIES: Sentence Level

D. Discuss these questions in a small group. Use a dictionary to clarify word meanings if needed.

1. Which of these possible discoveries could resolve the debate about the authorship of Shakespeare's plays? (You may choose more than one.)

   a. copies printed before Shakespeare's death

   b. handwritten copies of the plays

   c. a book by someone in Shakespeare's time crediting him with the plays

   d. Shakespeare's diary

2. Think about your own writing in a language other than your native language. Which of these aspects of writing is the hardest for you? Why?

    a. finding exactly the right word

    b. correctly using the vocabulary you already know

    c. finding a native-like organization

    d. developing a style that keeps your readers interested

3. What might be some consequences of each situation? Which consequences are good and which are bad? Explain your answers.

    a. investing your money in a new business

    b. investing your time as a volunteer

    c. reading a depressing book

    d. going against protocol by wearing shorts to school or work

---

The verb *depress* means "cause to sink to a lower position." It can be used in many contexts:

Physical	He **depressed** the DELETE key to erase the document.
Business	The warm weather **depressed** the skiing industry for months.
Economics	During a **depression**, the unemployment rate increases.

The most common context is emotional. *Depressed* can mean simply sad or it can refer to a medical condition in which chemicals in the brain are out of balance, causing constant sadness.

Sad	He's very **depressed** about his grades. He might not finish the class.
	That film was **depressing**. Let's do something fun to lighten the mood.
Clinical	She has suffered from **depression** since she was a teenager.
	It's hard for someone who is clinically **depressed** to hold a job.

E. On a scale from *1* (most depressing) to *10* (not at all depressing), rate each of these things. Discuss your ratings in a small group.

.... 1. romantic movies

.... 2. a big family gathering

.... 3. the last day of school

.... 4. spending the day alone

.... 5. looking at pictures from your childhood

.... 6. remembering a relative who is now dead

.... 7. seeing your former girlfriend or boyfriend with someone else

F. Look at these arguments for and against considering a writer's personal life when evaluating his or her work. Restate each idea in your notebook, using some form of the word in parentheses. Then, write a paragraph that expresses your own opinion. Try to use as many target words as possible in your work. Be prepared to read your paragraph or debate this issue in class.

For	Against
A writer's basic view of the world is determined by his or her experiences. Of course this affects the writer's approach. (*indicate*)	The same experience can affect different writers differently. We can only guess at its influence. If our guesses are wrong, we may misunderstand the work. (*reluctant*)
Writers often base the characters in their works on real people. Unless we know who these people are and what relationships they had to the author, we can't fully understand the work. (*text*)	A literary character is never exactly like a real person. Thinking about real people when you read keeps you from seeing the character as the author has developed it. (*persist*)
You can only know whether an author's handling of a topic is reliable by evaluating his or her experience. For example, Herman Melville's writing about whales in *Moby Dick* seems more reliable once you know that Melville used to work on ships. (*adequate*)	Reliability doesn't necessarily depend on experience. A good author can write about something well without ever experiencing it. For example, an author can easily write about emotional problems without having them. (*depression*)

G. Self-Assessment Review: Go back to page 43 and reassess your knowledge of the target vocabulary. How has your understanding of the words changed? What words do you feel most comfortable with now?

WRITING AND DISCUSSION TOPICS

1. The Oxford–Stratford debate is not the only disagreement about the authorship of important literary works. Do you know of any others? If so describe the controversy. Why is there doubt about who wrote the work(s)?

2. Joseph Conrad could work as a seaman on British ships without knowing much English. Describe two or three other foreign-language settings in which someone might be able to work without knowing much of the language.

3. Think of written works in the language you know best. Can you tell when a work in that language has been written by a foreigner? If so, how? Describe some specific features that make a piece of writing seem foreign.

4. Is a professionally translated book or play just as good as the work in its original language? What are some advantages and disadvantages of reading a work in translation?

WEATHER WARNINGS

In this unit, you will

- ➲ read about the role of weather experts in court and about a surprisingly dangerous type of snowstorm.
- ➲ practice reading and understanding charts and graphs.
- ➲ increase your understanding of the target academic words for this unit:

assist	energy	interval	previous	section
coherent	ensure	orient	reinforce	strategy
core	exhibit	phenomenon	route	

SELF-ASSESSMENT OF TARGET WORDS

Think carefully about how well you know each target word in this unit. Then, write it in the appropriate column in the chart.

I have never seen the word before.	I have seen the word but am not sure what it means.	I understand the word when I see or hear it in a sentence.	I have tried to use the word, but I am not sure I am using it correctly.	I use the word with confidence in either speaking or writing.	I use the word with confidence, both in speaking and writing.

MORE WORDS YOU'LL NEED

blizzard: a snowstorm in which high winds make it very difficult to see

court: a location in which public arguments about legal issues take place

forecast: a prediction of future events; often used in reference to weather

hail: frozen rain that falls in hard, round balls, even in warm weather

BEFORE YOU READ

Read these questions. Discuss your answers in a small group.

1. What is the weather like at your school or university today? How do you know? What was it like on this date last year? If you don't know, how can you find out?

2. Name some ways in which weather affects business. In what ways is bad weather expensive?

3. How might weather play a role in solving crimes?

READ

This article explains how weather data is helping settle court cases.

The Weather Goes to Court: Forensic Meteorology

The witness testified that she had heard the defendant confess to stealing a car. She was sitting on a park bench, she said, when the defendant, speaking loudly and pointing forcefully toward the parking lot, told another man he had just "jacked that silver Toyota." She said she could easily overhear it because the defendant was standing only about 50 yards northeast of her. She knew it was him because he was on a small hill where she could easily see him. The prosecutor thanked her and she sat down.

It was the defense attorney's turn. His **strategy** was to make the jury doubt what they had just heard. He called a new witness, a meteorologist. People throughout the courtroom wondered: Why call a weather expert?

The expert confidently stated that it had been sunny with excellent visibility on the day in question. Weather records said so. Could the **previous** witness have seen the defendant talking? The weather would not have been a problem, the expert said. Could she have overheard what he said? "Well, the way she described it, probably not. The wind was a bit strong that day, out of the southwest at about 15 miles per hour. He was northeast of her and standing on a hill. Sound waves heading into wind get pushed upward. By the time they had traveled 50 yards, they would have been too high to reach her ears."

This case **exhibits** how meteorology can be considered a branch of forensic science. The term *forensics* comes from a Latin word that means "arguing for or against a position." In common modern usage it means "the practice of discovering material that can be used in court cases or other disputes." Sciences from anthropology to zoology have been put to forensic use. Forensic meteorology can contribute to the picture of the conditions surrounding a crime or an accident. Rather than providing a forecast of what the weather might be in the future, forensic meteorologists specialize in "backcasts" of what the weather was at a given time in the past.

Weather **phenomena** have been measured and carefully recorded for hundreds of years. In the United States, daily records of air temperature, sky conditions, precipitation[1], and wind are available for almost any inhabited place. What was the weather in New York like for George Washington's 1789 inauguration as the first president? Clear skies with a high

[1] *precipitation*: moisture from the air that falls to the ground, e.g., rain or snow

temperature of 59° Fahrenheit. Anyone with an Internet connection can find that information in five minutes, without any **assistance** from a highly paid meteorologist. An expert's true
60 value is presenting data to **orient** you to the general circumstances and then interpreting that data and pointing out possibilities. The expert analysis draws scattered facts together into a **coherent** picture.

65   For example, imagine that a farmer wants his insurance company to pay for storm damage to his crops. A large **section** of his cornfield has been flattened. Official records say hail fell that day. He blames the hail for the damage
70 to his crops, and his policy clearly covers hail damage. His insurance company disputes the **core** argument of his case—that the damage was done by hail. The company denies the claim. The farmer, moved to action by the prospect of
75 collecting tens of thousands of dollars, takes the company to court.

The insurance company calls in a forensic meteorologist. The company's lawyer shows photographs of the farmer's damaged corn-
80 stalks, which all fell to the ground in the same direction. The destructive **energy** of hail, she testifies, produces damage from above not from the side. She also says that sophisticated radar data show that the storm, as it passed over the
85 farm, lacked the strong updrafts needed to produce hail. Hail was recorded at the weather station 30 miles away, about 6 minutes before the storm reached the farm. But in that short **interval**, the character of the storm changed.
90 This evidence has given the judge strong doubts about the farmer's claim. These doubts are **reinforced** when the meteorologist explains that radar data also show an extremely strong burst of wind at the farm's location. The judge
95 eventually rules that the crop damage was caused not by hail but by wind. The farmer's policy does not cover wind damage.

The tools of forensic meteorology continually get more precise, more affordable, and easier
100 to use. Any eager entrepreneur who wants to start a weather-consulting business can buy and operate the necessary equipment. So what **ensures** that someone claiming to be a forensic meteorologist really is? Neither the
105 federal government nor any state officially licenses meteorologists. The best **route** to professional status is to earn the title of Certified Consulting Meteorologist from the American Meteorological Society (AMS). Experts with that
110 credential have demonstrated to the AMS that they know what they are doing and are honest. Those are very good qualities to have when you step up to the witness stand in a court of law.

READING COMPREHENSION

Mark each sentence as *T* (true) or *F* (false) according to the information in Reading 1. Use the dictionary to help you understand new words.

.... **1.** Sound waves have enough energy to travel straight through a strong wind.

.... **2.** Meteorologists often act as judges in court.

.... **3.** Forensic scientists discover and interpret evidence to use in court cases.

.... **4.** George Washington became president of the United States on a sunny day in New York.

.... **5.** Weather records for previous years are available only to certified meteorologists.

continued

.... **6.** Hail typically has a downward orientation, not a sideways orientation.

.... **7.** Only records at an official weather station can be introduced in court.

.... **8.** An insurance policy might cover one type of weather phenomenon but not another.

.... **9.** A forensic meteorologist must have a license from the federal or state government.

.... **10.** A professional organization certifies meteorologists to ensure that they have competency in the core areas of meteorological science.

READING STRATEGY: Reading Graphs

A reading text may include a chart or a graph to show relationships among ideas. A chart usually has vertical columns and horizontal rows. A graph looks more like a picture, such as a set of lines, an arrangement of bars, or a circle divided into sections.

Look at the graph showing average temperature and precipitation data for Minneapolis, Minnesota. Answer the questions that follow in your notebook. Compare answers with a partner.

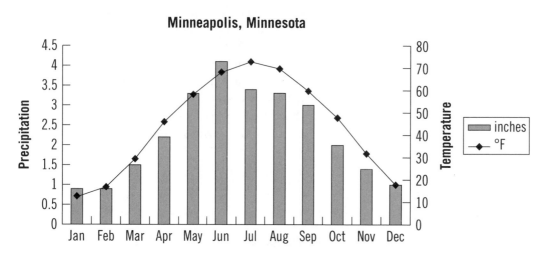

Minneapolis, Minnesota

1. What is the coldest month in Minneapolis?
2. What is the warmest month?
3. What is the wettest month?
4. What are the driest months?
5. In which months are the average precipitation levels the same?
6. In which two months are the average temperatures the same?
7. What is the relationship between average temperature and precipitation?
8. If you were going to visit Minneapolis, when would you go? Why?

STEP I VOCABULARY ACTIVITIES: Word Level

A. Read these excerpts from another article on meteorology. For each excerpt, cross out the one word or phrase in parentheses with a different meaning from the other three choices. Compare answers with a partner.

1. The study of weather (*extremes* / *events* / *phenomena* / *happenings*) before humans began recording events is called paleometeorology (PM), the prefix *paleo-* meaning "old."

2. Perhaps the best-known achievement of PM is the development of techniques for reading ice (*cores* / *routes* / *samples* / *specimens*) from the world's oldest ice fields.

3. Tubular drills penetrate hundreds of meters into solid ice. When they come back up, they contain long cylinders of layered ice, each layer exhibiting a distinct (*period* / *interval* / *time* / *strategy*) of atmospheric conditions.

4. In one layer, bubbles of a certain form of oxygen might indicate an especially warm set of years. Another layer may (*exhibit* / *display* / *orient* / *show*) flecks of volcanic ash from a period of many eruptions.

5. Ice cores cannot indicate weather from day to day, or even from one year to the next. Instead, they (*assist* / *reinforce* / *aid* / *help*) scientists in seeing long-term changes over periods of hundreds of years.

6. Ice cores are used with other indicators of climatic conditions to develop a(n) (*unified* / *coherent* / *engaging* / *integrated*) account of what happened on Earth previous to recorded weather data.

7. For example, many scientists claim that from about 800 CE to 1100 CE, the climate was unusually warm. Evidence of plant life, core samples of soil, erosion patterns in rocks, and accounts of human activity all (*indicate* / *reinforce* / *confirm* / *strengthen*) this claim.

8. The mild weather helped the Norse of medieval Scandinavia sail through ice-free North Atlantic waters to Greenland and Newfoundland. The end of the warm weather (*ensured* / *energized* / *guaranteed* / *made it certain*) that the Norse settlements in Greenland would become isolated and eventually disappear.

B. What did you do (or what do you usually do) in the interval between these events? List as many things as you can. Discuss your list with a partner. How similar are your results?

1. the interval between very cold weather and very warm weather

2. the interval between finishing one school year and starting another

3. the interval between the first and second acts of a play

4. the interval between one love interest and another

5. the interval between something bad you did as a child and your parent(s) finding out about it

6. the interval between sending an important text message and waiting for the reply

The word *strategy* means "plan of action." It is used mostly in the context of government or business, but individuals can also have personal strategies for accomplishing things.

C. Imagine you want to find out what the weather was like on the day and in the place your mother was born. Put a check (✓) next to the strategies you would use. For each strategy you check, be prepared to say how it might be useful and what difficulties it might present. Discuss your answers with a partner.

.... **1.** examine the rings of a tree trunk

.... **2.** talk to very old people

.... **3.** visit the headquarters of the National Weather Service

.... **4.** do an Internet search

.... **5.** visit the library at your school or university

.... **6.** talk to your mother or father

STEP II VOCABULARY ACTIVITIES: Sentence Level

Word Form Chart			
Noun	Verb	Adjective	Adverb
energy	energize	energetic	energetically

In this unit, *energy* refers to forces or sources of power in the environment. Heat, coal, gas, wind, and water can all be sources of energy.

*The **energy** from the storm originates in the Pacific Ocean.*

When *energy* is used to refer to people, it means "the ability to be very active" or "to activate something or something."

*People usually have less **energy** in hot weather.*

*The cool weather has really **energized** me to finish the work in the garden.*

D. Write answers to the questions in your notebook, using the word in parentheses. Refer to Reading 1 for information. Compare answers with a partner.

1. In the opening scenario of Reading 1, what did the witness say she saw? (*energetically*)

2. According to the meteorologist, why did the witness probably not hear the defendant? (*energy*)

3. Why did the farmer decide to take the insurance company to court? (*energize*)

4. Why does hail do damage to the hood of a car but not the tires? (*energy*)

5. Who can become a forensic meteorologist? (*energetic*)

6. What should a meteorologist understand in order to be certified? (*energy*)

Word Form Chart

Noun	Verb	Adjective	Adverb
assistance assistant	assist	assisted	....
coherence	....	coherent	coherently
exhibit exhibition	exhibit	....	....
phenomenon (plural: phenomena)	....	phenomenal	phenomenally
section	section	sectional	sectionally

E. Read these sentences about some research on lightning. Then, go back and answer the questions that appear after each piece of information in your notebook. Use a target word from the chart above in your answers. Be prepared to read aloud or discuss your answers in class.

1. Researchers at Duke University have begun analyzing data for a hypothesis about the connection between lightning and the emission of high-energy gamma rays coming from Earth's own atmosphere.

   What will be the result of all the separate pieces of data?

2. Natural emissions of gamma rays—extremely energetic forms of electromagnetic radiation—are usually caused only by high-energy events in space.

   What usually causes emissions of gamma rays?

3. In 1994, scientists detected gamma rays that showed signs of originating near Earth's surface. And researchers quickly found evidence that those emissions were connected to lightning.

   What was special about the gamma rays found in 1994?

4. With the help of the National Science Foundation, Duke tried to define that connection. They found that, on average, one of these TGFs (terrestrial gamma-ray flashes) occurs about 1.4 seconds before an actual lightning flash.

   How did Duke get the money and resources to pursue their research?

5. The exact cause of these TGFs remains unclear. The researchers have begun looking at different areas of thunderclouds. They believe something happens near a cloud top during a thunderstorm to create extremely powerful electron beams.

   How are the scientists examining thunderclouds?

6. Whatever causes TGFs probably depends on atmospheric occurrences found only in the tropics.

   Why wouldn't scientists be able to find TGFs in Canada?

BEFORE YOU READ

Read these questions. Discuss your answers in a small group.

1. Have you ever been in a snowstorm? If so, where? What were conditions like during the storm? If you haven't experienced a snowstorm, what do you think it would be like?

2. Hundreds of people die each year in snowstorms. What are the most dangerous aspects of snowstorms? What can people do to stay safe in these storms?

3. Consult a map of North America and locate these places: the Pacific Ocean; the Rocky Mountains; Alberta; Minnesota. What do you know about these areas?

READ

This article is about a small but dangerous type of snowstorm.

Alberta Clippers

Snowstorms come in many forms, and storm experts know them by many names, such as the "Panhandle Hook" or the "Nor'easter." Each type of storm exhibits certain traits, depending
5 on where it gets started and where it goes. One type of snowstorm known throughout North America is the Alberta Clipper. On a satellite photo, a clipper looks small, but it can be at least as dangerous as a storm three times its size.
10 As the name suggests, the storms form over the western Canadian plains, usually in the province of Alberta. Once they form, they move fast. It is not unusual for a clipper to travel its route from western Canada to the Atlantic in about 72
15 hours. It is also not unusual for several clippers to line up one after another, striking the same areas over and over again.

The original energy for an Alberta Clipper comes from the Pacific Ocean. During a normal
20 winter, storms come ashore over western North America continually, at two- or three-day intervals. A storm that comes in over British Columbia or southeastern Alaska will drop most of its moisture on the coastal rain forests.
25 But the low-pressure area at the core of the storm may hang together as it crosses the Rocky Mountains. The storm, still a coherent swirl around a small center, enters very cold air over the North American high plains.
30 Now quite dry, the low-pressure system wraps the cold air into itself. It then rides southeast on a stream of air coming down from the arctic. As it moves south, it encounters slightly warmer air and slightly more moisture. These both
35 feed into the storm and reinforce it. Warmer air moves northward along the eastern (front) edge of the clipper. Cold air slices southward on the western (back) half. The boundary between these two air masses, called a cold front, is very
40 sharply defined. Once the cold front passes, the air temperature may plunge 30 degrees Fahrenheit in just an hour.

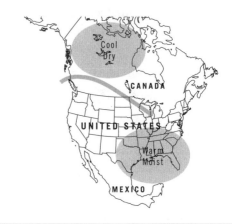

Most of the snow in an Alberta Clipper falls in the warm (eastern) section of the storm. In a typical clipper, this is not very much—perhaps two or three inches of light, dry snow. But even such small amounts can cause a lot of trouble once a clipper's true force is felt. As the temperature falls behind the cold front, vicious winds of at least 35 or 40 miles per hour create ground blizzards. No new snow falls during a ground blizzard, but those two or three inches that fell earlier are whipped up into blinding swirls. Visibility drops to almost zero.

Ground blizzards routinely produce a phenomenon called "black ice." Blasts of polar air instantly freeze any moisture on the previously warm roads. The ice is smooth and clear, but it is called "black" because the dark surface of the road is visible beneath it. On ice so smooth, automobile tires have nothing to grab, and the vehicle starts to slide out of control. Trying to brake or steer will only ensure that the car whips around unpredictably as it slides. The best strategy for the driver is to do nothing and hope to glide to a stop without hitting anything.

Many cars keep sliding until they hit deep snow at the side of a road. The people inside the car are usually shaken but not seriously hurt.

Still, they are in grave danger. As the ground blizzards continue and snow piles up around their cars, people may begin to panic. It's cold. They can't see more than three feet beyond the car. They wonder if help will ever come. Fear and stress may cause them to make bad decisions. Some have made the mistake of walking off into the blinding snow to search for help. They then become disoriented and helpless. At the very best, such people are found frostbitten but still alive in some hollow in the snow. More often, their bodies are found by search dogs after the wind settles down.

In the clear morning after one Alberta Clipper raced through west-central Minnesota, state troopers and rescue crews pulled people from cars half-buried along Highway 55. Most were alive and in generally good health. Twelve people, however, did not survive the storm. Five of them were members of a single family on their way to get some pizza when the clipper struck. At the height of the storm, rescuers on snowmobiles had found the family car and offered assistance. They offered to take the children to safety and then come back for the adults. The father, thinking unclearly, refused to let anyone go. It wasn't such a bad storm, he said. They would just wait it out.

READING COMPREHENSION

Mark each sentence as *T* (true) or *F* (false) according to the information in Reading 2. Use the dictionary to help you understand new words.

.... 1. Alberta Clippers are a common type of snowstorm in North America.

.... 2. They are called "clippers" because they move fast.

.... 3. The route of an Alberta Clipper is from east to west.

.... 4. Heavy snow is the most dangerous aspect of an Alberta Clipper.

.... 5. Black ice forms after the temperature drops with the passing of a clipper.

.... 6. It is unwise to try steering a car that is sliding on black ice.

.... 7. If your car is stuck during a clipper, you should wait a short interval until the blizzard calms down, then go in search of help.

.... 8. Conditions during a clipper can cause people to think unclearly.

READING STRATEGY

Alberta Clippers: The Facts				
Stage of Storm	Air Temperature	Snowfall	Wind	Hazards
Before	26–30	0	West, 5 mph	....
Early	31–35	2–3 inches	South, 15 mph	Possibly some low visibility
Middle	30–0	0–1 inch	Northeast to North, 35–40 mph or higher	High winds, cold, low visibility, roads becoming icy
Late	0–5	0	North to Northwest, dropping from 40 mph to 5–10 mph	Low visibility, snowdrifts, icy roads, disabled cars, bitter cold
After	0–5	0	Northwest, 2 mph	Ice, snowdrifts, blocked roads, buried objects, bitter cold

Note: Temperatures are in degrees Fahrenheit. Figures for temperature, snowfall, and wind are approximate readings for a location in the northern Midwest in late January.

A. Use the information in the chart above to answer these questions.

1. Between which two consecutive stages does the greatest temperature difference occur?

....

2. What is the snowiest stage in an Alberta Clipper event?

....

3. Describe the changes in wind direction related to an Alberta Clipper event.

....

4. At what stage(s) is someone most likely to have a storm-related car accident?

....

B. Now, look at the table again and come up with three questions to ask a partner.

....

....

....

STEP I VOCABULARY ACTIVITIES: Word Level

A. Complete the sentences about "thundersnow" using the target vocabulary in the box. Use each item one time. The synonyms in parentheses can help you.

disoriented	exhibit	reinforces
energy	phenomenon	section

1. One Saturday morning in March 1993, many people in the eastern United States woke up to the sounds of high winds and crashing thunder. They were .... by what they heard, and they ran to their windows to (confused) see flashes of light amidst heavy, blowing snow. Thunder and lightning during a blizzard?

2. Most snowstorms do not produce thunder and lightning because there is not enough .... in the atmosphere. (power)

3. Although it is an unusual occurrence, thunderstorms can accompany a snowstorm. This weather .... is known as *thundersnow*. (happening)

4. The troposphere is the .... of the atmosphere closest to (part) Earth's surface. An extremely powerful winter storm system, if accompanied by intensely cold air in the upper regions of the troposphere, can produce thundersnow.

5. Although thundersnow is uncommon in most of the eastern United States, storms in the Great Lakes region do .... it. (display)

6. Areas in the Rocky Mountains also experience thundersnow, particularly during the spring and fall. The great height of the western slopes of the mountains .... the rising air. (strengthens)

B. Many academic words are also considered formal words. Which of the target words in this unit (see the chart on page 57) are more formal synonyms for these informal words? Be sure to use the right forms of the target words.

Informal	Formal
1. earlier	....
2. show	....
3. strengthen	....
4. way	....
5. main	....
6. break (time period)	....

C. Read the sample sentences that feature forms of the word *orient*. **Then, answer the questions below in your notebook, using a dictionary as suggested. Compare answers with a partner.**

> **a.** Before the school year starts, new students attend a one-day *orientation*.
> **b.** After getting off the roller coaster, Andrea felt dizzy and *disoriented*.
> **c.** Keep heading north. If you get confused, that bright star can *orient* you.
> **d.** Children can attend the workshop, but it's really more adult *oriented*.

1. Put a check (✓) next to the word closest in meaning to *orient*. Consult your dictionary before you answer.

   .... direct .... configure .... expose .... mentor

2. Match the form of *orient* in each sentence with one of the meanings below.

> confused   informational meeting   point in the right direction   suitable

   a. ....   **c.** ....

   b. ....   **d.** ....

3. Look at the sample sentences in your dictionary for *orient* and its forms. Who or what is being oriented or disoriented in each of those samples?

4. Does *orient* have any forms that are not used in the sample sentences in the box above? If so, what are they? Consult your dictionary.

STEP II VOCABULARY ACTIVITIES: Sentence Level

> The adjective *coherent* refers to things fitting together in a logical order, or being clear and easy to understand. The noun is *coherence*.
>
> *The police have a **coherent** plan in place for rescuing people after a snowstorm.*
>
> To indicate the opposite, you can say that something is *incoherent* or that it *lacks coherence*.
>
> *His essay on gamma rays has a lot of good information, but it **lacks coherence**.*

D. For which of these things is coherence very important? Put a check (✓) next to them. Then, write a few sentences in your notebook for each item explaining why coherence is or is not important. Discuss your choices in a small group. Refer to your explanations when you argue your point.

.... 1. a children's storybook

.... 2. directions to a business

.... 3. a painting

.... 4. the way you study for a test

.... 5. city streets

.... 6. a friend's story about her vacation

.... 7. the arrangement of items in a grocery store

.... 8. music

The verb *exhibit* means "to show something to the public." The noun forms in this context are *exhibition* and *exhibitor*.

*The people who were rescued **exhibited** signs of disorientation.*

*She **exhibited** her paintings in the New Artists **Exhibition** downtown, which had more than 100 **exhibitors** in all.*

In legal proceedings, such as trials and lawsuits, the pieces of physical evidence that each side presents are referred to as *exhibits*.

*The lawyer for the defense presented the broken fencepost as **Exhibit** A. He entered about twenty **exhibits** into evidence in all.*

E. You are the lawyer for the defense. Read the summary of the facts in this case and answer the questions that follow on this and the next page.

Case summary: Your client, Mr. Logan, was driving home from work. While en route, a snowstorm started and he became disoriented. He drove into the yard of a neighbor, Mr. Simms, and knocked down his fence. Mr. Logan continued back to the road and went home. The next day, he went to Mr. Simms and explained what happened. Logan assisted Mr. Simms in repairing the fence and even reinforced it to ensure that it would be strong all winter. He paid for all materials. Two months later, Mr. Simms's lawyer called your client to tell him that Simms was suing him for $5,000.00. Simms claims that repairing the fence is not enough. His yard will need work in the spring, which Logan should pay for, and Logan should be punished for his bad driving.

1. What strategy will you use in this case?

   a. Prove Mr. Logan is an excellent driver. This is one minor mistake that he has done his best to correct. He should not be punished in any way.

   b. Present Mr. Logan as an equal victim in this situation. Both parties suffered because of weather phenomena that they could not control.

   c. Paint Mr. Simms as a greedy man who is only trying to get money from Mr. Logan.

   d. Argue that the interval between accident and claim was too long. Any claim against any person should be made in a timely manner. If the judge allows this, then anyone who ever made a mistake could be sued at any time in his or her life, which is unfair.

   e. Other: ....

2. What three points best support your strategy?

   a. ....

   b. ....

   c. ....

continued

3. What evidence could you use to reinforce each point?

   a. ....

   b. ....

   c. ....

4. What exhibits will you present to support the evidence?

   ....

   ....

   ....

5. How will you argue your case to the judge? Bring all the points and evidence together into one coherent argument (a summary of your case). Write your argument to the judge in your notebook.

F. Read the argument you prepared in activity E to a partner to make sure it is coherent. Revise your argument according to your partner's feedback. Then, read your argument aloud in class. Your classmates will act as the jury and vote on your case.

G. Self-Assessment Review: Go back to page 57 and reassess your knowledge of the target vocabulary. How has your understanding of the words changed? What words do you feel most comfortable with now?

WRITING AND DISCUSSION TOPICS

1. Most forensic meteorologists are private parties who sell their services. One side or another hires the meteorologist to say certain things in court. What are some problems that may result?

2. The availability of weather data via the Internet raises the question, "Are forensic meteorologists really necessary?" What do you think? Give reasons for your opinion.

3. Technological improvements have revolutionized many aspects of meteorology. Still, forecasters are not really confident about any predictions they make for more than three or four days in the future. What do you think might improve their forecasting ability? Do some research about this issue on the Internet if possible.

4. Snowstorms can be dangerous, but so can other types of bad weather. Choose another weather phenomenon and explain why it is dangerous.

5. When a bad snowstorm is forecast, how should a driver prepare? If you have no experience driving in the snow, do some research on the Internet, or talk with people who have had the experience.

BRAIN FOOD

In this unit, you will

- ⊃ read about some ways that food can affect psychological and cognitive functions.
- ⊃ learn to summarize a text.
- ⊃ increase your understanding of the target academic words for this unit:

affect	compile	journal	paradigm	prospect
allocate	coordinate	mental	period	react
commit	discrete	overall	promote	team

SELF-ASSESSMENT OF TARGET WORDS

Think carefully about how well you know each target word in this unit. Then, write it in the appropriate column in the chart.

I have never seen the word before.	I have seen the word but am not sure what it means.	I understand the word when I see or hear it in a sentence.	I have tried to use the word, but I am not sure I am using it correctly.	I use the word with confidence in either speaking *or* writing.	I use the word with confidence, both in speaking *and* writing.

MORE WORDS YOU'LL NEED

cognitive: related to thought and learning

intolerant: unwilling or unable to accept certain behavior or circumstances

diet: the set of foods a person usually eats

BEFORE YOU READ

Read these questions. Discuss your answers in a small group.

1. Name three or four foods you often eat even though you know they're not good for you. Why are they unhealthful? Why do you eat them anyway?

2. Name three or four foods you eat that are healthful. Why are they healthful? Do you like the way they taste?

3. Have you ever felt a significant improvement in your mood or in your concentration after a meal or snack? What do you think caused this effect?

READ

This excerpt from a nutrition manual explains the psychological benefits of eating certain fats.

Fat for Brains

As the old saying goes, you are what you eat. The foods you eat obviously **affect** your body's performance. They may also influence how your brain handles its tasks. If it handles them
5 well, you think more clearly and you are more emotionally stable. The right foods can help you concentrate, keep you motivated, sharpen your memory, speed your **reaction** time, defuse stress, and perhaps even prevent brain aging.

10 **Good and bad fat**

Most people associate the term *fat* with poor health. We are encouraged to eat fat-free foods and to drain fat away from fried foods. To understand its psychological benefits, however,
15 we have to change the **paradigm** for how we think about fat.

The first step is gaining a better understanding of fat. Instead of conceiving of it as one thing, we have to recognize it as several
20 **discrete** types of a similar compound. Not every fat is your enemy. Fats, of the right kinds and in the right amounts, are among your best friends. It is smart to **commit** to a balanced-fat diet, not to a no-fat diet.

25 Fats are broadly classified as either "saturated" or "unsaturated." Most foods that contain fat contain both kinds, in varying proportions.

Foods that are high in saturated fats include meat, butter, and other animal products.
30 In general, saturated fats are solid at room temperature. Foods high in unsaturated fats include vegetable oils, nuts, and avocados. Unsaturated fats, if separated out, are usually liquid at room temperature.

Foods high in saturated fats

Foods high in unsaturated fats

The key to health is to **allocate** a percentage of your fat intake to each type of fat. Saturated fat in moderate amounts poses no problem. In general, you will be fine if less than 20 percent of the fats you consume are saturated. Beyond that level, saturated fat may **promote** heart disease and perhaps some types of cancer. A diet high in saturated fat can also make you depressed and antisocial and impair your general **mental** performance. Unsaturated fats should make up the bulk of your fat intake. But beware. Unsaturated fats are especially high in calories and could cause weight problems. The smart approach is to keep your **overall** fat intake low and make sure that most of it is in the form of unsaturated fats.

Fatty acids

Keeping your fat intake too low, on the other hand, could also be dangerous. Fat in food is broken down into chemicals called fatty acids. The body uses them for many purposes. They go into all hormones. They are critical to body metabolism. And they are part of the outer membrane of every cell in the body, including those in the brain. You need these fatty acids in order to stay physically healthy and mentally sharp.

Of the many fatty acids the body uses, two are called "essential fatty acids" (EFAs). Your diet must contain foods that provide them, because the body cannot make them on its own. The most important are omega-3 fatty acids. They are crucial for the proper development of the human brain. All brain-cell membranes need to refresh themselves continually with new supplies of omega-3s.

North Americans are famous for consuming too much saturated fat and too much total fat. They also consume far too little food that provides omega-3s. The vegetable oils most commonly used in cooking—corn, safflower, and sunflower oils—have almost no omega-3s.

Using canola (rapeseed), soy, and walnut oils, which have ample omega-3s would be far more healthful. And the old saying about fish being brain food is true. Fish is rich in omega-3s, especially in one, called DHA, that is identical to a material in the membranes of nerve cells. People allergic to or intolerant of fish can get their DHA from several sources, including leafy green vegetables, sesame seeds, or egg yolks.

Omega-3s and the brain

There is evidence that DHA plays a big role in the intellectual performance of humans. In one well-respected study, premature infants were fed either standard American infant formula or breast milk. Results showed that the children given breast milk had significantly higher IQs. The researchers also **compiled** data on the children for eight years after the initial feeding **period**. Through all that time, the children never lost this mental advantage. The research **team** concluded that the IQ superiority resulted exclusively from DHA, a known component of breast milk. Most American baby formulas do not contain any DHA.

In psychology and physiology **journals**, articles routinely confirm the value of omega-3 fatty acids. One published study demonstrated that fish oil reduced the degree of brain damage in cats experiencing stroke. A study by researchers at the University of Pittsburgh showed that adults with low levels of omega-3s in their bodies were far more depressed, pessimistic, and impulsive than those with normal or high levels. This evidence improves the **prospects** for treating depressed patients effectively. Many therapists now say they are determined to **coordinate** psychological therapy with dietary therapy in order to rely less on drugs.

As research continues to show, new ways of thinking about fat can open the door to better physical, mental, and emotional health.

READING COMPREHENSION

Mark each sentence as *T* (true) or *F* (false) according to the information in Reading 1. Use the dictionary to help you understand new words.

.... **1.** Foods affect a person's moods and motivation.

.... **2.** Ideally, more people should commit to no-fat diets.

.... **3.** At room temperature, you could pour unsaturated fat out of a bottle.

.... **4.** It is not healthful to eat a very large amount of unsaturated fat.

.... **5.** Omega-3 fatty acids promote intellectual development.

.... **6.** Breast milk is a better source of DHA than infant formulas.

.... **7.** Research journals reported that people with a lot of omega-3 fats in their systems were very depressed.

.... **8.** Patients with psychological problems should coordinate their therapy so that it includes dietary as well as psychological treatment.

READING STRATEGY: Summarizing

A summary of a reading text should be short. It should cover all the main ideas and give an overall idea of the text. It may include some important supporting points but it should NOT emphasize smaller points. Think of a summary as an outline in paragraph form (see Unit 4 for more on outlining).

The best summaries come from a good understanding of the whole reading. There are, however, some techniques that can help you prepare a good summary:

- State the main idea of the whole text in your first sentence.
- Look at headings to help you identify some of the main ideas.
- Scan paragraphs to identify their topics. Do not simply look for "topic sentences." Not every paragraph has one, and those that exist are not always easy to locate.
- For each main point, add one reason from the text that explains why it is important.

A. Use the headings in Reading 1 and any obvious paragraph clues to decide whether each of these topics belongs in a summary of the reading. Put a check (✓) next to those items that should be included. Discuss your choices with a partner.

.... a balance of fats

.... brain cells

.... canola oil

.... DHA

.... fish

.... IQ and depression

.... obesity

.... omega-3s

.... psychological therapy

.... saturated and unsaturated fats

.... the United States

.... the University of Pittsburgh

B. Write a one-paragraph summary of Reading 1 using the main ideas you identified. Your summary should be no more than 80 words long.

STEP I VOCABULARY ACTIVITIES: Word Level

A. Read these excerpts from another article on the psychological effects of food. In each excerpt, cross out the one word or phrase in parentheses with a different meaning from the other three choices. Compare answers with a partner.

1. Many studies have tried to determine whether Attention Deficit Hyperactivity Disorder (ADHD) is (*influenced* / *affected* / *caused* / *impacted*) by the foods children eat. The goal is to test claims that ADHD symptoms, like poor concentration and impulsive behavior, are triggered by something in food.

2. If they are, eliminating these "provoking substances" would presumably (*complete* / *encourage* / *promote* / *facilitate*) healthier behavior.

3. Some researchers have focused on diets that eliminate many food additives and even ban some foods. Others study "few-foods" diets—those that (*convert* / *divide* / *distribute* / *allocate*) a child's total calorie intake among only a few types of food.

4. One study found that, (*overall* / *in total* / *as a whole* / *finally*), behavior problems increased in 69% of the children after they were given food containing colorings or other possible provoking substances.

5. In another study, the research (*team* / *sponsor* / *group* / *squad*) monitored brain activity by looking at electroencephalograms (EEGs).

6. First, they recorded brain activity during (*times* / *periods* / *sections* / *intervals*) when the children were on a few-foods diet with no suspected provoking substances. Then they took EEGs when the children ate only foods with suspected provoking substances.

7. After the researchers (*wrote* / *gathered* / *put together* / *compiled*) and compared the EEGs, they noted large increases in some brain-wave activity during the second stage of the test.

People and organizations usually have a plan for how they are going to use their resources—they *allocate* their resources. Notice that you allocate something *to* or *for* something else.

*We **allocated** 20% of our budget **to** advertising.*

The noun form is *allocation,* and the adjective is *allocable* (or *allocatable*).

*The highest priorities typically get the greatest **allocation** of resources.*

*Some **allocable** resources are money, fuel, space, time, and attention.*

B. During a typical week, how much time do you allocate to these activities (not how much time you spend doing them, but how much time you plan for them)? Estimate the time in hours. Compare answers with a partner.

1. watching TV ....
2. hanging out with friends ....
3. reading (for pleasure) ....
4. playing video games ....
5. going to the movies ....
6. studying ....
7. using the Internet ....
8. playing team sports ....

C. Which of these activities require you to coordinate with other people? Put a check (✓) next to them. Then, decide what type of coordination is necessary (schedules, access, meeting times, etc.). Compare answers with a partner.

Type of coordination

.... 1. watching TV ....
.... 2. hanging out with friends ....
.... 3. reading (for pleasure) ....
.... 4. playing video games ....
.... 5. going to the movies ....
.... 6. studying ....
.... 7. using the Internet ....
.... 8. playing team sports ....

STEP II VOCABULARY ACTIVITIES: Sentence Level

Word Form Chart			
Noun	Verb	Adjective	Adverb
commitment	commit	committed	....

D. The word *commit* has several different meanings and uses, depending on context. Match each phrase with its example sentence. Then, rewrite the example sentences using the matching phrase.

a. commit a crime

b. commit suicide / homicide

c. not commit yourself

d. be totally committed to someone or something

e. have a commitment

f. have commitments

g. honor a commitment

h. get out of a commitment

i. make a (financial) commitment to

j. a lack of commitment

_i_   **1.** "I promised to give money every month to the Diabetes Research Foundation."

"*I made a financial commitment to* the Diabetes Research Foundation."

.... **2.** "I can't meet at that time because I've promised to do something else then."

....

.... **3.** "All she thinks about is her daughter."

....

.... **4.** "He suffered from depression for many years then finally killed himself."

....

.... **5.** "His leaving early shows that he doesn't care about this team enough."

....

.... **6.** "The government has fulfilled the promise to allocate more money to the school lunches program."

....

.... **7.** "He went to prison for carrying out several illegal acts."

....

.... **8.** "She thinks she can come tomorrow, but she won't promise until she talks to her sister."

....

.... **9.** "They would love to take a vacation but they have responsibilities that need their attention."

....

.... **10.** "He's not really sick. He's just trying to rid himself of a promise he made."

....

Word Form Chart

Noun	Verb	Adjective	Adverb
....	affect	affected unaffected	....
mentality	....	mental	mentally
....	....	overall	....
promotion promoter	promote	....	promotionally
prospect prospects	....	prospective	prospectively
reaction	react	reactive	....

E. Read more information about how diet affects cognitive functioning. Then, in your notebook, restate information using the word(s) in parentheses. Be prepared to read aloud or discuss your sentences in class.

1. Chemical compounds called antioxidants may become more important in your diet as you get older. A number of studies have suggested that they help maintain memory skills and other cognitive functions in older adults. (*mentally*)

2. Antioxidants in the body trap damaging chemicals, known as free radicals, and limit the damage they can do. (*react* or *reaction*)

3. Free radicals cause damage to tissues in nearly every part of the body. Their general effect on the body is partly responsible for the slow decline we call "aging." (*overall*, *promote*)

4. One of the most disturbing aspects of aging is what happens to the brain. Aging can cause slower reaction times, memory loss, and a dulling of the senses. (*affect*)

5. Some people seem to have improved their chances of staying sharp in old age by eating foods that contain adequate amounts of antioxidants. (*prospects*)

6. Several studies of older patients taking antioxidant pills, however, showed no significant differences between these patients and older persons who took no supplements. (*unaffected*)

BEFORE YOU READ

Read these questions. Discuss your answers in a small group.

1. War often causes widespread hunger. Why does this happen?

2. Have you ever seen someone suffering from long-term undernourishment, perhaps because of poverty or disease? Have you ever seen a picture of such a person? Describe the way he or she looked.

3. Have you ever been very hungry or very thirsty? How did that affect your mood? Did it affect your ability to think? How?

READ

This excerpt from a nutrition textbook tells the story of the first clinical study of the effects of starvation on physical and mental functioning.

The Minnesota Starvation Experiment

On November 19, 1944, 40 healthy young men entered the Laboratory of Physiological Hygiene at the University of Minnesota. They were ready to embark on a grueling medical experiment.
5   The men had responded to a brochure that asked: "Will You Starve That They Be Better Fed?" World War II was coming to a close, and the Allied forces[1] needed to know how to deal with starving people in areas of Europe and Asia
10 ruined by the war.

Basic design

In 1944, the prospect of finding healthy young men to volunteer for such an experiment was dim. Many were overseas serving in the military.
15 However, many conscientious objectors—those who refused to serve in the war for religious or moral reasons—remained in the United States doing various types of community service. The government eventually allowed them to
20 volunteer for medical experiments. About 400 men volunteered for the Minnesota research, of whom 40 were eventually selected.

The study took place in three discrete stages. The first, starting in November 1944,
25 was a "standardization" period of 3 months. So they could be observed under non-stressful conditions, the men received a substantial 3,200 calories of food per day. This was followed by a 6-month semi-starvation period, beginning on
30 February 12, 1945, in which they received only 1,800 calories per day. The semi-starvation diet reflected what was available in the war-torn areas of Europe—potatoes, turnips, rutabagas, dark bread, and macaroni. The final 3 months
35 were a nutritional rehabilitation period.

Throughout the study, participants were given various housekeeping and administrative duties within the laboratory. They were also allowed to participate in university classes and activities. The
40 participants were expected to walk 22 miles (35.4 kilometers) per week and to expend 3,009 calories per day.

The good days

Those selected to participate were a well-
45 educated group. All had completed some college coursework. Many took advantage of the opportunity to take more courses at the

[1] *Allied forces*: the term for the group of nations in World War II consisting primarily of the United States, the United Kingdom, the Soviet Union, and China

University of Minnesota during the experiment. Initially, their blue pants, white shirts, and sturdy walking shoes were all that distinguished them from other people on campus. During the standardization period, the men felt well-fed and full of energy. Many initially volunteered for local charities, participated in music and drama productions, or otherwise contributed to community projects in the area.

Semi-starvation

On the first day of semi-starvation (February 12, 1945), the men sat down to a meal that included a small bowl of hot cereal, two slices of toast, a dish of fried potatoes, a dish of Jello, a small portion of jam, and a small glass of milk. Each was now allocated less than half the calories he was used to consuming. The men ate their meals together in Shevlin Hall on the campus. Participants were supposed to lose 2.5 pounds (1.1 kg) per week to reach the desired 25% weight reduction by the end of the semi-starvation period.

As semi-starvation progressed, the men became irritable and intolerant of one another. Many of them kept journals during the experiment, which recorded their feelings and reactions as they happened. One of the men, Carlyle Frederick, later remembered "noticing what's wrong with everybody else, even your best friend. Little things that wouldn't bother me before or after would really make me upset." Another, Marshall Sutton, noted, "We were impatient waiting in line if we had to, and we'd get disturbed with each other's eating habits at times. We became, in a sense, more introverted[2], and we had less energy." The men reported feeling cold much of the time and asked for extra blankets even in the middle of summer.

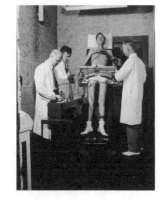

They experienced dizziness, extreme tiredness, muscle soreness, hair loss, reduced coordination, and ringing in their ears. They felt weak mentally as well as physically. Several were forced to quit their university classes because they simply didn't have the energy or motivation to attend and concentrate. Food became an obsession, and several of the men said they had lost all interest in women and dating.

The men became more noticeable around campus as they began to show visible signs of starvation—sunken faces and bellies, protruding ribs, and swollen legs, ankles, and faces. Despite the challenges of starvation, there was a determination among the men that somehow kept them committed. When each of the 36 men who completed the experiment was asked if he had ever considered withdrawing, the reply was repeatedly firm and succinct: "No."

Slow recovery

The three-month rehabilitation period began at the end of July 1945 and continued until October 20, 1945. With the end of the war that summer, the results of the experiment were becoming increasingly relevant. How should the recovering populations of Europe and Asia be fed? As the experiment showed, the answer was far more complex than simply, "Give them food." Many of the men reported that, overall, the rehabilitation period was the hardest of all. Their strength came back only slowly, and many were depressed by this delayed recovery. Their feelings of hunger remained. They continued to be dizzy, confused, and irritable.

The research team eventually published these results in academic journals. They also prepared a relief worker's manual that focused on the psychological effects of food deprivation. The experiment helped create a new paradigm for understanding starvation. Previously, starvation was seen as only a physical thing. The experiment showed that it dramatically alters personality and that nutrition directly and predictably affects the mind.

---

[2] *introverted*: quiet and shy, concerned only with one's own thoughts and feelings

READING COMPREHENSION

Mark each sentence as *T* (true) or *F* (false) according to the information in Reading 2. Use the dictionary to help you understand new words.

.... 1. The Minnesota Starvation Experiment involved soldiers from the Allied Forces.

.... 2. The experiment compiled data to help deal with starvation problems in Europe and Asia.

.... 3. In the first stage of the experiment, the men ate so much they became obese.

.... 4. In the second stage of the experiment, the men continued walking 22 miles per week.

.... 5. In the third stage of the experiment, the men quickly regained their previous health.

.... 6. The men's journals record that they became depressed and irritable as they began to lose weight.

.... 7. Eventually, the participants lost all mental motivation to continue in the experiment.

.... 8. The study showed that rehabilitating starved populations involved more than food supplies.

READING STRATEGY

A. Using subheadings and paragraph clues, plan a 100-word summary of Reading 2. Outline your plan in your notebook, but do not write the summary yet. Discuss your plan with a partner.

B. Keeping in mind your partner's comments, revise your plan. Then write a 100-word summary of Reading 2 in your notebook.

STEP I VOCABULARY ACTIVITIES: Word Level

A. Many academic words are also considered formal words. Which of the target words in this unit (see the chart on page 71) are more formal synonyms for these informal words? Be sure to use the right forms of the target words.

Informal	Formal
1. length of time	....
2. put together	....
3. magazine	....
4. set aside	....
5. separate	....
6. push	....

B. Complete the sentences about nutrition and child development using the target vocabulary in the box. Use each item one time. The synonyms in parentheses can help you.

affect	mental	promote
compiled	overall	prospect
coordination	paradigm	reacted

.... **a.** At the other end of the weight spectrum, obesity may negatively

.... a child's image of himself or herself. This may lead
(have an impact on)
to lower academic performance for overweight children.

.... **b.** Data .... by government agencies suggest that providing
(gathered together)
breakfast to school-age children has lessened these problems.

.... **c.** Nutritionists use the term *food-insecure* to mean "not sure whether healthy

meals will be consistently available." By emphasizing a child's attitudes

and expectations instead of actual food intake, this reflects a change in the

prevailing .... among experts.
(way of thinking)

.... **d.** One study showed that children in food-insecure households scored

lower on arithmetic tests, were more likely to have repeated a grade, and

.... more violently when teased by other children.
(responded)

.... **e.** Other studies have found that child hunger raises the .... of
(possibility)
severe behavior problems and long-term anxiety/depression.

.... **f.** Overweight children often lag behind others in developing physical

.... and stamina. Because they cannot keep up with others
(integrated movement)
at play, they are more likely to be socially isolated than children who are not

overweight.

.... **g.** Some schools reportedly have tried to .... better test scores
(increase the chances of)
for the school .... by providing healthier school lunches.
(as a whole)

.... **h.** Under-nutrition in children probably affects their ....
(related to the mind)
development. Presumably, a lack of food deprives the brain of essential

nutrients. Also, difficulties involving food probably have emotional

consequences.

C. Put the sentences in activity B into a logical order to describe some effects of nutrition on child development. (More than one order may be possible.) Read your sequence to a partner.

D. Read the sample sentences that feature forms of the word *coordinate.* Then, answer the questions below in your notebook, using a dictionary as suggested. Compare answers with a partner.

> **a.** The school superintendent *coordinates* the operations of 12 elementary schools.
> **b.** Members of the choir are required to wear color-*coordinated* outfits for performances.
> **c.** Bad nutrition can affect a person's hand–eye *coordination*, making it difficult to play sports or music instruments.
> **d.** The camp hires an athletic *coordinator* to run its sports programs.

1. Put a check (✓) next to the word closest in meaning to *coordinate*. Consult your dictionary before you answer.

   .... command   .... organize   .... reminisce   .... recur

2. Each of these sentences indicates that things were coordinated. What are they?

   a. ....

   b. ....

   c. ....

   d. ....

3. Look at the sample sentences in your dictionary for *coordinate* and its forms. What is being coordinated in each of those samples?

4. Does *coordinate* have any forms that are not used in the sample sentences in the box above? If so, what are they? Consult your dictionary.

STEP II VOCABULARY ACTIVITIES: Sentence Level

> The adjective *discrete* describes something that is separate from or independent of other things of the same type. The adverb form is *discretely*.
>
> *Fats can be divided into **discrete** types.*
>
> Note the spelling of *discrete*, and do not confuse it with another adjective, *discreet*, which means "careful not to attract attention and cause embarrassment."

E. Rewrite each of these sentences in your notebook using *discrete*. Then, go on to provide the information introduced in each sentence. Compare results with a partner.

1. A person's life can be divided into a few significant time periods.

2. A college career usually follows a series of levels.

3. Nurses are responsible for varied operations within a hospital.

4. The Minnesota Starvation Experiment was broken into three distinct stages.

5. The people in my life promote my health and well-being in different ways.

Many medical and psychological experiments like the Minnesota Starvation Experiment are controversial and cause strong reactions both for and against them. Critics say that some of them are cruel, immoral, or mentally and physically harmful. Defenders of these experiments say they are necessary and justifiable because the knowledge they provide helps everyone.

F. Read this summary of an actual medical experiment. What are the two most extreme reactions (for and against) that you can imagine? What is your own reaction? Do you think the experiment was justified? Why or why not? Write a separate one-paragraph summary of the reactions you have listed. Be prepared to read aloud and discuss your work in a small group.

Experiment: In 1984, a doctor tried implanting the heart of a baboon into a baby girl with a severely deformed heart. A baboon was killed to provide the heart. The baby girl died, as she probably would have without the operation.

Reaction for: ....

....

Reaction against: ....

....

Your reaction: ....

....

G. Self-Assessment Review: Go back to page 71 and reassess your knowledge of the target vocabulary. How has your understanding of the words changed? What words do you feel most comfortable with now?

WRITING AND DISCUSSION TOPICS

1. When designing a diet for yourself or another person, what information would you need? How would you gather the data? How would you compile it? Are there any paradigms you would follow?

2. Cognitive and emotional difficulties are often partly caused by—or made worse by—an inadequate diet. ADHD is one such difficulty. What other illnesses or disorders can result from poor nutrition? Go online to research this topic, then present a summary of your results.

3. Some people claim that the dietary problems faced by modern societies have arisen because we no longer eat fresh ingredients from local farms. People in earlier times ate better because the food they bought was more nutritious than what most people now eat. Do you agree with this point of view? Why or why not?

4. What are you committed to in your life? Describe your personal commitments and explain why you made these commitments.

5. Have you ever kept a journal? Why or why not? What is the value of writing about your life as it happens?

Unit 7 Geology

ROVING CONTINENTS

In this unit, you will

⮑ read about the movement of the large plates that make up the Earth's outer layer, the crust.

⮑ make inferences and draw conclusions.

⮑ increase your understanding of the target academic words for this unit:

accommodate	comprehensive	fluctuate	nuclear	reverse
aid	displace	integrate	random	rigid
community	evolve	intermediate	restrain	transform

SELF-ASSESSMENT OF TARGET WORDS

Think carefully about how well you know each target word in this unit. Then, write it in the appropriate column in the chart.

I have never seen the word before.	I have seen the word but am not sure what it means.	I understand the word when I see or hear it in a sentence.	I have tried to use the word, but I am not sure I am using it correctly.	I use the word with confidence in either speaking *or* writing.	I use the word with confidence, both in speaking *and* writing.

MORE WORDS YOU'LL NEED

continent: a large landmass; the seven continents are Africa, Antarctica, Asia, Australia, Europe, North America, and South America

theory: a systematic explanation of how something might work

BEFORE YOU READ

Read these questions. Discuss your answers in a small group.

1. What continent do you live on now? Does it connect with other continents? Did you ever live on (or visit) another continent?

2. Have scientists discovered any evidence that the climate on your continent was once very different from what it is now? What caused the change(s)?

3. Name two parts of the world that experience a lot of volcanic eruptions or earthquakes. What do you think causes these events?

READ

This introduction to a chapter in a geology textbook explains the basic ideas behind the theory of a long-ago supercontinent on Earth.

Pieces of a Puzzle: The Evidence for Pangaea

1   In geology, a *plate* is a large, **rigid** piece of solid rock. The Earth's surface is built of about 40 plates, called *tectonic plates*—some as large as continents and others only a few hundred miles across. Modern geology has shown that these tectonic plates move in relation to each other. Such movement is possible because the plates float on top of the *mantle*, the layer of molten[1] rock between the planet's outer crust and its dense **nucleus**, called the *core*. Even before this theory of plate tectonics became accepted, many in the geological **community** believed Earth's continents had moved during the history of the planet. They were right, but they faced great opposition.

2   Until the 1700s, most Europeans explained the origins of Earth's bodies of water and landmasses in terms of "catastrophism." According to this way of thinking, a few sudden, violent events (catastrophes), such as the great flood described in the Bible, periodically **transformed** the Earth's surface. Then, a revival of science in Europe **restrained** the imaginations of geographers. Catastrophism was **displaced** by "uniformitarianism," a term derived from the word *uniform*. According to this point of view, the forces we see shaping the Earth now are the same forces that shaped it in the past. Since most of the processes we see are slow and gradual, we can assume that, for the most part, Earth's surface was shaped slowly and gradually.

3   The belief that continents have not always been in their present positions was common long before the 20th century. In 1596, the Dutch mapmaker Abraham Ortelius suggested that the Americas were "torn away from Europe and Africa... by earthquakes and floods." As evidence, he pointed out that, if you tried putting Africa and South America together, they would fit almost like two puzzle pieces. The big opening along Africa's western coast would easily **accommodate** the "hump" in South America's eastern coastline.

4   Later versions of the scenario said that the arrangement of today's continents gradually **evolved**. In 1912, a scientific explanation, called the *theory of continental drift*, was proposed by a German meteorologist named Alfred

---

[1] *molten*: melted, usually used to describe rock, such as volcanic lava

Lothar Wegener. He contended that all of Earth's landmasses were once joined in a single supercontinent, which he called *Pangaea* (from the Greek *pan-*, meaning all or complete, and *Gaea*, the mother of the Earth). According to Wegener's theory, about 200 million years ago, Pangaea began to split apart. One of Wegener's biggest supporters, Alexander Du Toit, proposed an **intermediate** stage. He said that Pangaea first broke into two large continental landmasses: *Laurasia* in the northern hemisphere and *Gondwanaland* in the south. Laurasia and Gondwanaland then continued to break apart into the various smaller continents that exist today.

5   Wegener's theory was based in part on the remarkable fit of the South American and African continents noticed by Ortelius three centuries earlier. He and his supporters also offered other pieces of evidence. For example, fossils of an ancient plant called *Glossopteris* were found throughout the southern continents—Africa, Australia, Antarctica, and South America—and in India. If all these continents had not once been joined, *Glossopteris* would probably not have spread so far. And if Antarctica had not once been closer to the equator, the plant would not have grown there at all.

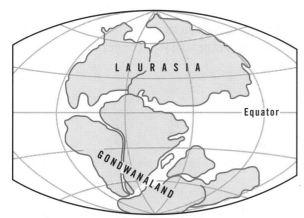

Pangaea breaks into two masses, then into the continents we know today.

6   Geological structures on today's separated continents also offered evidence. Some mountains in South Africa are structurally identical to mountains in eastern Brazil. The coal deposits of Britain match deposits in the Appalachian Mountains of eastern North America. A band of red sandstone stretches from northeastern Europe, through Greenland, and into Canada. These similarities seemed too numerous to be **random** coincidences.

7   Wegener's theory, especially his ideas about Pangaea, took things too far for most of the scientific **community.** They might be willing to accept an Africa / South America split, but not split after split and then migration. Their strongest objections centered on the question, "How?" Some developed detailed explanations for why it was physically impossible for continental rock to move across the ocean floor. Such objections were entirely reasonable, and Wegener's theory had no good answer.

8   Finally, in the late 20th century, the theory of plate tectonics came to the **aid** of the theory of continental drift. It offered the **comprehensive** explanation of landmass movement that Wegener had been unable to provide. New evidence made it hard to believe that the continents were *not* moving. The floor of the Atlantic Ocean was found to be spreading apart. New discoveries showed that the planet's magnetic field is not constant. It **fluctuates** over very long time periods, and has clearly shifted several times. The theory's system of plates moving on molten rock offered a believable answer to the question, "How?" It **integrated** pieces of evidence ranging from volcanic activity to the formation of mountains to the distribution of fossil plants. It showed that Pangaea not only could exist but probably did. It also said that the trend toward separation would eventually **reverse.** The continents would drift together again and form a new supercontinent.

READING COMPREHENSION

Mark each sentence as *T* (true) or *F* (false) according to the information in Reading 1. Use the dictionary to help you understand new words.

.... **1.** The earth's large landmasses continually move around the globe.

.... **2.** Earth's crust is solid, but the other parts of the planet are liquid.

.... **3.** Maps in the 1600s showed that Africa and South America might once have fit together.

.... **4.** Alfred Wegener's theory was essentially the same as Ortelius's theory.

.... **5.** *Glossopteris* fossils are widespread because the continents were once all at the equator.

.... **6.** Some bands of rock appear on several separate continents.

.... **7.** The biggest criticism of Wegener's theory was that it failed to explain the advantages of continental movement.

.... **8.** The theory of plate tectonics solved the biggest problems posed by the theory of continental drift.

.... **9.** Continents on either side of the Atlantic are getting farther from each other.

.... **10.** Someday, the continents might all be joined together again.

READING STRATEGY: Making Inferences

When you make an inference, you use clues in a reading to understand something the author has not directly stated. The reading implies it, and you infer it. An inference is a conclusion that you draw from the information presented in the reading.

Read the paragraph indicated again. Then, select the one or two statements that can be most strongly inferred from each paragraph. Compare selections with a partner and explain your choices.

1. Paragraph 1:

    a. There are more small tectonic plates than large ones.

    b. The top layer of the mantle is liquid.

    c. The continents were formed from material in the mantle.

2. Paragraph 2:

    a. Catastrophists believed the Earth should not change.

    b. Catastrophists believed religion should not interfere with science.

    c. Catastrophists believed forces we now witness were not enough to shape the Earth.

3. Paragraphs 4 and 5:

    a. Wegener formulated a theory about meteorology that also worked for geology.

    b. Wegener was not the only scientist of his time who thought Pangaea once existed.

    c. Wegener went on expeditions to explore the continents in the Southern Hemisphere.

4. Paragraph 7:

    a. Wegener's theory was weak in some respects.

    b. Wegener's opponents were catastrophists.

    c. Wegener's opponents could accept that, on a rare occasion, a landmass might break into two.

STEP I VOCABULARY ACTIVITIES: Word Level

A. Read these excerpts from an article on tectonic plates. For each excerpt, cross out the one word or phrase in parentheses with a different meaning from the other three choices. Compare answers with a partner.

1. *Geodesy* is the study of the size and shape of the Earth. Over thousands of years, the tools of the field have (*fluctuated / developed / evolved / progressed*) so that now we can use geodetic measurements to track the movement of tectonic plates.

2. Because plate motions happen all over the globe at the same time, only satellite-based methods can give a truly (*all-inclusive / comprehensive / accurate / thorough*) view of them.

3. In the late 1970s, these space-based techniques completely (*improved / changed / altered / transformed*) the field of geodesy.

4. Of the space-based techniques, the Global Positioning System (GPS) has provided the most (*aid / assistance / truth / help*) to scientists studying the movements of the Earth's crust.

5. By repeatedly measuring distances between specific points, geologists can determine if there has been significant (*displacement / restraint / movement / repositioning*) among the plates.

6. For example, scientists now know that earthquakes and volcanic eruptions along the lines between plates do not occur (*rigidly / by chance / randomly / haphazardly*).

7. Space-geodetic data have already confirmed that the present-day rates and directions of plate movement (*fit in / integrate / harmonize / evolve*) well with the geologists' estimates.

> The word *integrate* means "to join things so that they become one thing or fit together." Often, sentences with *integrate* mention the individual things (or people) and the larger thing that eventually includes them.
>
> His theory **integrated** the work of several scientists in different fields of study.
>
> The new students slowly **integrated** into the social groups on campus.

B. What smaller parts might integrate into each of these larger units? Compare answers with a partner.

1. an army
2. a public park
3. the European Union
4. a transportation network
5. an all-star soccer team
6. a neighborhood

C. Which of these things do you think should be rigid? Which are less rigid or can fluctuate depending on the situation? Write *R* for those that you think should be rigid and *F* for those that can fluctuate. Discuss your answers in a small group.

.... 1. bedtime for small children

.... 2. financial agreements between friends

.... 3. financial agreements between family members

.... 4. transport schedules (bus, train, plane)

.... 5. a teacher's grading system

.... 6. religious beliefs

.... 7. political views

STEP II VOCABULARY ACTIVITIES: Sentence Level

Word Form Chart			
Noun	Verb	Adjective	Adverb
transformation	transform	transformative	....

D. Answer these questions in your notebook. Use each form of *transform* at least once in your answers. Refer to Reading 1 for information. Compare sentences with a partner.

1. What is the most significant way Earth's landmasses have changed since the days of Pangaea?
2. As scientific thinking became more advanced in Europe, how did explanations of Earth's geology change?
3. How did continental drift affect Antarctica?
4. What role did the theory of plate tectonics play in the debate about continental movement?
5. What big change is likely in the arrangement of Earth's continents?

Word Form Chart			
Noun	Verb	Adjective	Adverb
accommodation	accommodate	accommodating	accommodatingly
displacement	displace	displaced	....
evolution	evolve	evolved evolving evolutionary	....
restraint	restrain	restrained restraining	....
reverse reversal	reverse	reverse	(in reverse)

E. Read another excerpt related to plate tectonics. Then, in your notebook, restate information using the word(s) in parentheses. Concentrate on main ideas and leave out the less important details. Be prepared to read aloud or discuss your sentences in class.

1. A growing number of geologists are letting their thoughts roam a few hundred million years in the future. (*restrain*)

2. Using the principles of plate tectonics, they try to guess how the arrangement of Earth's continents will change between now and 250 million years from now. (*evolve*)

3. Dr. Christopher R. Scotese, of the University of Texas Arlington, predicts that the current continents will slowly join again, creating a new supercontinent, *Pangaea Ultima*. (*evolution*)

4. He and other geologists agree about other likely changes. As Africa moves north toward Europe, it will squeeze the Mediterranean Sea out of its location. A rugged range of Mediterranean Mountains will take its place. (*displace*)

5. An immense new landmass containing present-day Africa, Europe, and Asia— *Afrasia*—will form. Australia and Antarctica will run into it. Only a small basin will be left for a vastly smaller Indian Ocean. (*accommodate*)

6. South America will move north, pushing aside the islands of the Caribbean, until northern Venezuela bumps into southern Florida. The two Americas will together head west toward eastern Afrasia. (*displace*)

7. Scotese predicts that, about 200 million years from now, the westward-moving Americas will change direction and head east toward the other side of Afrasia. The Atlantic Ocean will disappear. (*reverse* and *displace*)

8. Other geologists believe nothing will keep the Americas from moving west, as they are now. "My guess," said Dr. Sergei A. Pisarevsky of the University of Western Australia, "is that the Pacific should disappear." (*restraint*)

9. Many geologists agree that Pangaea Ultima will eventually form, and there are many different scenarios for how it might happen. When you're guessing about the next 250 million years, you have to be prepared for surprises. (*accommodation* or *accommodate*)

READING 2

BEFORE YOU READ

Read these questions. Discuss your answers in a small group.

1. Find the African countries of Eritrea, Ethiopia, and Djibouti on a map. What do you know about these countries or this area of the world?

2. On the map of Africa, what geological features indicate where a tear might be located on the Earth's crust?

3. How do oceans form?

READ

This online newspaper article examines a major geological event occurring in East Africa.

An Ocean Waiting to Happen

The nomads[1] were terrified. For a week in September of 2005, the ground shook violently. Cracks opened up in the soil, swallowing goats and camels. Smoke rose out of the dark splits
5   in the ground. After retreating to the hills, the nomads saw chunks of glassy rock burst randomly through the Earth's crust "like huge black birds" and fly almost 100 feet into the air. A mushroom cloud of ash dimmed the sun for
10 three days. At night the new crater[2] breathed flashes of fire.

"They had experienced earthquakes before but never anything like this," said Atalay Ayele, a scientist at Addis Ababa University,
15 who interviewed the Afar tribespeople in this isolated corner of northeastern Ethiopia. The Afar community explained it by saying God was angry with them.

Dr. Ayele and his colleagues knew the area
20 was geologically unstable, but the number of strong earthquakes was exceptional. There were 162 quakes measuring more than 4 on the Richter scale[3] in just two weeks—a quake measuring 5 on the scale releases
25 as much energy as the nuclear explosion that destroyed Hiroshima in World War II. All this made Ayele's team suspect that something extraordinary had happened deep underground.

30 When satellite data for the region became available, they showed that huge forces had just transformed East Africa. Here in the Afar desert, one of the hottest and driest places on Earth, a new ocean was evolving. For the
35 first time, observation of an event of this sort was possible, aided by a satellite. Images from the European Space Agency's Envisat satellite showed that a huge rift, 40 miles (64 kilometers) long and up to 26 feet (8 meters) wide, had
40 opened deep in the Earth's crust. The tear was created by a violent upsurge of molten rock. This magma pushed in along a break where two plates of the Earth's crust meet. The magma displaced both plates, pushing them aside and apart.

45 Tim Wright, a geologist at the University of Leeds who interpreted the satellite results, was astonished by the images and what they pointed to. "The process happening here is identical to that which created the Atlantic Ocean," he said.
50 "If this continues we believe parts of Eritrea, Ethiopia, and Djibouti will sink low enough to allow water to flow in from the Red Sea."

---

[1] *nomad*: a member of a community that moves seasonally and has no permanent home
[2] *crater*: a large hole in the ground formed by natural processes
[3] *Richter scale*: the unit of measurement for earthquakes

Teams from the United Kingdom, France, Italy, and the United States have mounted expeditions to Afar. This is the region described by the explorer Wilfred Thesiger in the early 20th century as a "land of death." Satellites now give comprehensive views of what he meant. From above, you can see vast, rigid, black tongues of cooled lava reaching out into the desert sands. Rust-colored volcanoes stand open and gaping, their lids blown off. There are so many fissures[4] and faults[5] where the ground has opened and slipped that the Earth's skin looks like elephant skin.

The moon-like geography reflects what lies beneath. Afar stands at the junction of three tectonic plates, which meet at unstable fault lines. The Nubian and Somali plates run along the Great Rift Valley. The Arabian plate branches out to the north. The boundaries of these plates continually fluctuate as the upwelling of magma underneath pushes them around.

Earth's tectonic plates are constantly shifting—usually by only a few centimeters a year. Adjacent plates can slide past one another, as occurs along the San Andreas Fault, in California. The plates can also collide. India's collision with the landmass to the north started its integration with the Eurasian continent. This process forces the crust upward and creates mountain ranges, such as the Himalayas.

[4] *fissure*: a small crack
[5] *fault*: a large, deep crack in the Earth's crust

Or the reverse could happen. Plates can also pull apart, causing continents to break up and oceans to form. Early in this process, as the distance between plates increases, the Earth's crust stretches and thins out. Magma rises up, eventually cracking the thinned crust, and the plates drift apart. Between the fault lines, the crust, now heavy with cooled magma, sinks to form a deep valley, often below sea level. The formation of this depression is an intermediate stage in the birth of an ocean. A bowl now sits ready to accommodate water that rushes in from a nearby sea as soon as there is an open channel.

This is how the Atlantic was formed, separating Africa and Eurasia from the Americas. And this is what scientists believe is happening in Afar as the Arabian, Nubian, and Somali plates pull apart. Parts of the region have already sunk to more than 100 meters (328 feet) below sea level. Only the highlands east and north of the Danakil Depression restrain the Red Sea from rushing in. Eventually, erosion or quakes will create a break in the highlands, and the depression will quickly become an ocean floor. The new sea is predicted to be formed within about a million years. The complete separation of the Nubian and Somali plates along the Great Rift Valley could take ten times as long. At that time, Africa will lose its distinctive horn as the Somali Plate heads east.

READING COMPREHENSION

Mark each sentence as *T* (true) or *F* (false) according to the information in Reading 2. Use the dictionary to help you understand new words.

.... 1. During the 2005 earthquakes, pieces of rock flew up randomly out of the ground.

.... 2. Water from the Red Sea has rushed into the Afar region.

.... 3. A rift is a kind of opening.

.... 4. Three tectonic plates come together in the Afar region.

continued

.... 5. Before the 2005 earthquakes, the Afar region could accommodate farms.

.... 6. Despite the region's remoteness, the effects of the 2005 quakes have been extensively studied.

.... 7. Satellite photos of the Afar region show that a hole many miles long opened up in 2005.

.... 8. Scientists believe magma will rise up between the tectonic plates and displace them, pushing them farther apart.

.... 9. The Atlantic Ocean is the only thing restraining the new ocean from forming.

.... 10. Residents of Afar hope the new ocean will soon help relieve the extreme heat in the region.

READING STRATEGY

An author's choice of language can imply feelings or attitudes. Read these excerpts from Reading 2 and complete each implication that follows. Infer the adjective that best describes what the author means. Four of the adjectives will not be used. Check your dictionary for the meanings of new words. Compare answers with a partner.

accurate	incompetent	perceptive
avoidable	inevitable	unscientific
difficult	misleading	useful

1. The Afar community explained it by saying God was angry with them.

   Implication: The beliefs of the Afar community were ....

2. All this made Ayele's team suspect that something extraordinary had happened deep underground.

   Implication: Ayele's team is ....

3. This is the region described by the explorer Wilfred Thesiger in the early 20th century as a "land of death." Satellites now give comprehensive views of what he meant.

   Implication: Thesiger's description was ....

4. Images from the European Space Agency's Envisat satellite showed that a huge rift, 40 miles (64 kilometers) long and up to 26 feet (8 meters) wide, had opened deep in the Earth's crust.

   Implication: Envisat was ....

5. Eventually, erosion or quakes will create a break in the highlands, and the depression will quickly become an ocean floor.

   Implication: The formation of an ocean is ....

STEP I VOCABULARY ACTIVITIES: Word Level

A. Complete the sentences about Africa's Rift Valley with the target vocabulary in the box. The synonyms in parentheses can help you.

> accomodated   displacement   an intermediate
> aided   evolving   restrain
> community   fluctuated

.... **a.** "We are incredibly fortunate to have the Rift Valley," Leakey says, because that system has been .... over the last 20 million years."
(forming)

.... **b.** During the course of its formation, the rift's new basins ....
(made room for)
water from rivers and seas, water that carried lots of sediment with it.

.... **c.** Leakey has had the good fortune to live in .... period of
(middle)
the Rift Valley's history. The Eritrean and Ethiopian portions of the rift, in particular, are between an opening-up phase and a flooding phase.

.... **d.** Leakey says the continuing .... of land along the rift makes
(moving aside)
erosion possible in previously buried sediments, exposing new fossils.

.... **e.** Maeve Leakey, of East Africa's most famous family of fossil-hunters, considers herself lucky to have worked in the Rift Valley. She can barely .... herself as she describes the importance of the rift.
(control)

.... **f.** She also points out that "many of the rift sites, like Turkana, are badlands, which cannot be cultivated and are not threatened with buildings and concrete." Members of the scientific .... are the only humans
(group with shared interests)
with a reason to spend much time there.

.... **g.** The Great Rift Valley runs from southern Lebanon to southern Africa's Zambezi Valley. Its dramatic geology has .... anthropologists
(made things easier for)
hunting for remains of distant human ancestors, especially in Eritrea, Ethiopia, Kenya, and Tanzania.

.... **h.** The sediments buried the corpses of animals in the area, fossilizing bodies and animal bones. As water levels .... with changes in the
(went up and down)
landscape, the process repeated itself several times.

B. Put the sentences in activity A into a logical account of Maeve Leakey's observations. (More than one order may be possible.) Read your sequence to a partner.

C. Read each of these pairs. What are some intermediate stages between the members of the pair? Write as many as you can in your notebook. Compare lists in a small group and discuss your ideas.

1. child / adult
2. college graduate / professor
3. office assistant / company president
4. blueprint for a house / a livable residence
5. running one mile a day / running a marathon
6. falling in love / getting married
7. buying a camera / showing your movie to an audience
8. reading a recipe / serving dinner to family or friends

D. Read the sample sentences that feature forms of the word *accommodate*. Then, answer the questions below in your notebook, using a dictionary as suggested. Compare answers with a partner.

> **a.** As our family grew, my parents had to keep building additions onto the house to *accommodate* us all.
>
> **b.** Making *accommodation* for Jim's disability was not hard—a ramp at the front door, some new bathroom fixtures, and that's it.
>
> **c.** The proposal is quite *accommodating* to the opposing party's demands.
>
> **d.** He *accommodated* the press a great deal, giving interviews and posing for pictures.

1. Put a check (✓) next to the word closest in meaning to *accommodate*. Consult your dictionary before you answer.

   .... suit   .... access   .... compose   .... embrace

2. Each of the sentences in the box above indicates that something was accommodated. What was it?

   a. ....

   b. ....

   c. ....

   d. ....

3. Look at the sample sentences in your dictionary for *accommodate* and its forms. What is being accommodated in each of those samples?

4. Does *accommodate* have any forms that are not used in the sample sentences in the box above? If so, what are they? Consult your dictionary.

STEP II VOCABULARY ACTIVITIES: Sentence Level

> Some of the changes the Earth has undergone have been enormous. Some of them have been beneficial, some harmful, and some both, depending on which people you consider. For example, the Medieval Warm Period was certainly beneficial to the Vikings, who were able to explore farther than ever before. It was not so great, however, for the people the Vikings conquered during this period.

E. Each of these situations describes a big event or change on the Earth. How might the change be beneficial? How might it be harmful? Who does (or did) it affect and how? Write a few sentences for each item in your notebook, using at least two of the target words in parentheses, in any form, in your answers. Be prepared to read aloud or discuss your ideas in class.

1. The 10 hottest years, as measured by worldwide average temperatures, have occurred since 1998. There is no longer much serious doubt that the climate of the planet is getting warmer. (*fluctuate, reverse, random, transform*)

2. In 1991, a huge volcanic eruption at Mt. Pinatubo in the Philippines threw massive amounts of ash into the air. This hung in the atmosphere worldwide for most of the following 12 months and prevented sunlight from reaching the Earth's surface. The planet's average temperature in 1991 was almost one degree Celsius lower than normal. Worldwide, 1991 was the third-wettest year on record and had the third-coolest summer. (*aid, community, nuclear, transform*)

3. From 1963 to 1967, a new volcanic island, named Surtsey, formed off the southwest coast of Iceland. (*accommodate, community, displace, evolve*)

4. In human history, Africa's climate has become significantly drier. The Sahara Desert has expanded many times over, making it impossible for people to live, grow crops, or raise animals there. (*aid, displace, restrain, reverse*)

5. In 1908, a gigantic explosion occurred over the forests of Siberia in Russia. About 80 million trees were instantly flattened. People more than 100 miles away were knocked down by the shock wave from the explosion. It was probably caused by an asteroid vaporizing as it streaked through Earth's atmosphere. (*nuclear, random, rigid, transform*)

6. Until about 7000 years ago, a land bridge existed across the Bering Strait. It connected northeast Asia and what is now Alaska. It formed because a series of ice ages locked a great deal of water into glaciers, lowering sea levels. (*accommodate, evolve, integrate, intermediate*)

F. Not everyone accepts the theories of continental drift and plate tectonics. Look at these arguments for and against it. Restate each idea in your notebook, using some form of the word in parentheses. Then, write a paragraph that expresses your own opinion. Try to use as many target words as possible in your work. Be prepared to read your paragraph or debate this issue in class.

For	Against
There are many similarities among currently separate landmasses: similar fossils, similar mineral deposits, and similar geologic features. (*integrate*)	Landmasses are similar because they are all part of the same planet. There is no need to assume a supercontinent to explain these phenomena. (*random*)
Precise measurements have established that some pieces of Earth's crust are simply not in the same places they were 30 years ago. (*displace*)	Land moves all the time—sometimes slowly, sometimes quite fast—in such events as earthquakes and landslides. (*restrain*)
The theory of plate tectonics is scientific. It allows us to gather evidence, make predictions based on that evidence, and then test our predictions. It has done an excellent job of fitting in with observations experts have carefully recorded. (*accommodate*)	Almost every religion on Earth has an explanation of how the world took shape, and none of them mentions moving plates. Plate tectonics ignores wisdom that is thousands of years old. Scientists overestimate their abilities if they think truth has suddenly been discovered in the last 50 years. (*community*)

G. Self-Assessment Review: Go back to page 85 and reassess your knowledge of the target vocabulary. How has your understanding of the words changed? What words do you feel most comfortable with now?

WRITING AND DISCUSSION TOPICS

1. Look again at the events and changes in activity E on page 97. Choose one and do some research to find out more about it. Does your research change your mind about whether it was beneficial to anyone?

2. What geological phenomena or features are there in the area where you live? How might they have formed? How might they affect the climate of the region?

3. Plate tectonics may be useful in describing some other planets and some moons in our solar system. There is no evidence of present-day plate movement on any of these bodies, but it may have occurred in the past. On Mars in particular, more and more evidence suggests that there has been some movement of tectonic plates. What features would you expect to see on Mars if it once experienced the movement of tectonic plates? After you have taken your guesses, go online and search for "mars tectonic." Were any of your guesses correct?

CLICKS AND CLIQUES

In this unit, you will

⊃ read about how young people form social groups in different school environments.

⊃ annotate and highlight a text.

⊃ increase your understanding of the target academic words for this unit:

arbitrary	deviate	gender	institute	passive
clause	diverse	guarantee	intervene	so-called
converse	domain	inevitable	maximize	

SELF-ASSESSMENT OF TARGET WORDS

Think carefully about how well you know each target word in this unit. Then, write it in the appropriate column in the chart.

I have never seen the word before.	I have seen the word but am not sure what it means.	I understand the word when I see or hear it in a sentence.	I have tried to use the word, but I am not sure I am using it correctly.	I use the word with confidence in either speaking *or* writing.	I use the word with confidence, both in speaking *and* writing.

BEFORE YOU READ

Read these questions. Discuss your answers in a small group.

1. Have you ever had to share a room or an apartment with someone? Did you already know the person? Describe the experience.

2. What possible conflicts might roommates have? Would these conflicts be less likely to occur if the people knew each other already? Why or why not?

3. Have you ever looked for information about a friend or acquaintance on the Internet? If so, why? Did you find anything? Do you think it's okay to look people up without telling them?

READ

This newspaper article is about an Internet tool for finding out about college roommates.

Judging Roommates by Their Facebook Covers

Mailbox-watching is supposed to subside for high-school seniors after they receive their acceptance letters and make their college choices. Each summer, however, many an incoming
5   freshman[1] anxiously waits for the mailbox to produce another crucial envelope—the one holding the name of his or her future roommate.

Many people assume that college freshmen pick their dormitory roommates, as
10 upperclassmen are allowed to do. The **converse** is actually true. Very few colleges allow incoming freshmen any choice in dorm-room assignments. It's **inevitable** that students will worry about potential problems with a roommate—a
15 complete stranger. Students in the **so-called** millennial generation, in particular, are anxious about sharing a room with another person. Many have never shared a room at home. They are used to their rooms being their exclusive
20 **domains**.

For decades, residential-life offices have received late-summer telephone calls from worried students and parents. "People will read a name and address, and it fits into some category
25 in their head," says Sarah B. Westfall, dean of students at Denison University in Ohio. They expect a **diverse** student body at almost any college, but many students fear diversity as much as they look forward to it. Any indication that a
30 roommate's life **deviates** from the familiar can heighten a student's fear of the unknown. Online social-networking sites now allow students to get more of those indications than ever before.

According to college officials, many incoming
35 freshmen this year used Facebook and MySpace, two social-networking sites, to do research on their future roommates. Since everything happens anonymously[2], normally **passive** students can spring into investigative action
40 without having to approach a live person. On sites like these, anyone can post a profile of himself or herself free. Profiles can include photos, quotes, inside jokes, and lists of their favorite bands and TV shows. The idea is to
45 **maximize** your attractiveness to people with tastes similar to yours. MySpace has about 70 million registered profiles. Facebook now has 7.5 million registered users, at 2,200 colleges and 22,000 high schools.

---

[1] *freshman*: a first-year student at a four-year college, university, or high school
[2] *anonymous*: nameless, without identity

Roommates in their dorm room

Such profiles can help strangers break the ice before move-in day, but they can also cause alarm. A student's fondness for cartoons or punk rock can annoy a roommate before the two even meet. As a result, administrators are spending more time dealing with compatibility issues before students arrive. At some campuses, residential-life counselors have decided it's easier to prevent roommate problems than to **intervene** in them later. Their offices have prepared guides to using profiles wisely. They mail these guides out right from the start, in the same envelope as the notice of a roommate's identity.

Most students mistakenly believe the roommate-assignment system is **arbitrary**. The school might separate students by **gender**, they think, but beyond that it's a matter of chance. Actually, nearly every college prides itself on carefully considering each student's circumstances when assigning roommates. They don't **guarantee** roommates will get along, but they succeed much more often than they fail. They hate to see such careful work undone by a single click of a keyboard—especially since so many profiles are not exactly accurate.

Clauses in the user agreement for MySpace set some rules for profiles, but nothing in the agreement says they have to be true. Even students who use social-networking sites every day tend to forget that. For that reason, some schools have **instituted** "reality training" for social networkers. "We try to explain to them that there is a lot of posturing that goes on," one advisor says. "Students are trying to create an image that makes them seem fun and cool, and they post things that may or may not be true about themselves as a result." Admission officers also have students look at their own online profiles and ask "What kind of roommate do I look like?"

Some students say it's natural to form instant opinions when surveying their peers' profiles. Brandi, an incoming freshman at the University of Evansville, considers herself outgoing and easy to get along with. When she found out who her roommate would be, Brandi went to MySpace, where she found Sarah's profile. Her excitement quickly turned to disappointment.

"Her page was all pink, and I thought, 'Oh, gosh, we're not going to get along,'" says Brandi. "It said she was from California and into cheerleading, and I'm more into other sports. She just seemed really girly." Brandi found hope in Sarah's profile, however. Both students had listed Tim McGraw and Faith Hill as two of their favorite country-music singers. Sarah had also posted many photographs of herself with friends, who looked like the sort of people in Brandi's own clique. This convinced Brandi that her roommate was probably more similar to her than she thought.

So Brandi decided to give her future roommate a chance and sent her a message through MySpace. This started a conversation. Two telephone calls later, her first impression had changed. Sarah has two younger siblings, ages 15 and 17, just as Brandi does. And now that Brandi knows that Sarah took a lot of Advanced Placement classes[3] in high school, she no longer pictures her roommate as a ditzy California cheerleader.

"I think we're actually going to be really good friends," says Brandi.

---

[3] *advanced placement classes*: college level courses taught in high school

READING COMPREHENSION

Mark each sentence as *T* (true) or *F* (false) according to the information in Reading 1. Use the dictionary to help you understand new words.

.... **1.** Most universities arbitrarily match roommates in dorms.

.... **2.** Students could get information about future roommates even before social-networking sites became available.

.... **3.** Social-networking sites like MySpace were instituted by colleges and universities.

.... **4.** A social-networking profile can be designed to reflect one's tastes in music, favorite activities, and so on.

.... **5.** Anyone placing a profile on a social networking site must guarantee that the information is accurate.

.... **6.** Brandi considers herself a quiet, passive person and was afraid her future roommate would be too outgoing.

.... **7.** Music was the first common interest for Brandi and her roommate.

.... **8.** Brandi decided not to contact her new roommate because MySpace is not an accurate source of information.

READING STRATEGY: Highlighting and Annotating

After you read an article or chapter in a book, you may need to refer to the information again, for example, when you're studying for a test or writing an essay. Instead of copying the information you might need into a notebook, it is more efficient to *highlight* and *annotate* the reading.

Highlighting   using a bright marker to make important passages easy to see. You might also want to underline or circle parts of the reading.

Annotating   writing little notes to yourself in the margins of the reading

Highlight and annotate only the materials that you own!

Follow the directions to highlight and annotate Reading 1. You will need a colored marker and a pen or pencil. Then, with a partner, use your annotations to answer the questions that follow as quickly as you can.

- First, highlight all the names of individual people.
- Second, circle each name of a college or university. In the margin next to each, write its location.
- Third, highlight or underline any statistics or important data in the article (look for numbers and source citations).
- Fourth, as you read, highlight any unfamiliar words you encounter. In the margin next to each, write a short definition using your dictionary.

1. What school is Brandi going to attend? ....

2. Where is Denison University? ....

3. How many registered users does Facebook have? ....

4. How many different high schools are represented on Facebook? ....

5. What other networking site is mentioned in the article? ....

6. What does *posturing* mean in this context? ....

7. Which musicians do Brandi and Sarah both like? ....

8. Who is the dean of students at Denison University? ....

STEP I VOCABULARY ACTIVITIES: Word Level

A. Read this advice about behaving properly on a social-networking website. For each item, cross out the one word or phrase in parentheses with a different meaning from the other three choices. Compare answers with a partner.

1. Writing a comment to everyone on your list might be nice, but why are you doing it? Just to (*raise / maximize / display / increase*) the number of comments on your page? That's lame. You know who you are.

2. Ladies, if some (*deviant / cute / abnormal / weird*) guy who (1) you've never met and (2) has pictures of other girls on his page adds you to his friends list, don't add him back.

3. The fact that someone takes time to read and comment on your blogs is a(n) (*sure sign / guarantee / assurance / source*) of affection. It proves the person cares about your inner thoughts. Don't ignore these comments.

4. Having 500 people on your list of (*nominal / so-called / supposed / dear*) friends and only 20 comments is a sign that you have to pretend people like you. Add only people you know to your list. Be as popular as you are—or aren't.

5. Never respond to a private message with a comment in the public (*arena / realm / domain / dialect*). That's rude.

6. If you post a personal 100-question survey, there's one (*questionable / unavoidable / inevitable / certain*) result: Nobody will read it.

B. What is the converse of each of these things? Is there more than one? Read your answers with a partner and discuss (or converse about) the different possibilities.

1. love: ....

2. youth: ....

3. happiness: ....

4. success: ....

5. passivity: ....

6. inevitability: ....

The word *intervene* means "to come between" usually to prevent or solve a problem. Although it is similar to *interfere*, intervening is usually seen as helpful and interfering is considered impolite and annoying.

Sometimes, the difference between intervention and interference depends on the perspective of the people involved. For example, a passenger in a car might give the driver directions because he thinks the driver is lost. The passenger sees this as intervention, but the driver might see it as interference and be insulted.

C. In which of these situations would you intervene? Put a check (✓) next to them. Discuss your choices in a small group. Explain your perspective and decide whether the other people involved might consider your action (or inaction) interference.

.... **1.** Two students in your class are discussing whether there is a test tomorrow. One says there is, the other says there's not. You know that there is.

.... **2.** A confused-looking man you don't know is standing, with a map in his hand, on a street corner.

.... **3.** Some of your friends are playing soccer. You can see that players from the other team are tripping and knocking down players on your friends' team.

.... **4.** One of your friends is arguing with his or her father. You feel the father is being unfair.

.... **5.** Two of your cousins, who have very different political views, are arguing about politics.

.... **6.** As you are walking to a special dinner in a nice restaurant, you see that a car is stuck in some mud. One person is trying to drive while another person pushes, but the car is not moving.

.... **7.** You are watching your son's team play basketball, and the team is losing. You think you could give them some advice that would help them do better.

.... **8.** Four or five students are standing around another student, insulting him and pushing him around.

STEP II VOCABULARY ACTIVITIES: Sentence Level

Word Form Chart			
Noun	Verb	Adjective	Adverb
the converse	....	converse	conversely
diversity	diversify	diverse	diversely
guarantee	guarantee	guaranteed	....
inevitability	....	inevitable	inevitably
passiveness	....	passive	passively

D. Read another account related to college roommates. Then, in your notebook, restate the sentences, using the words in parentheses. Concentrate on main ideas and leave out details. Be prepared to read aloud or discuss your work in class.

1. Many college freshmen expect to socialize with their roommates, or even to be friends. They express surprise when things don't happen that way. (*conversely*)

2. This probably happens because few freshmen really know what to expect. With no prior experience of anything like a roommate relationship, they may think of it as a sort of official friendship set up by the university. (*guaranteed*)

3. And it may start out that way. Two people lost on a large campus, with no acquaintances outside the dorm, will naturally look to each other for a social foundation. (*inevitably*)

4. Soon, however, each one's social network spreads wider through classes, clubs, parties, and chance meetings. (*diversify*)

5. If both roommates succeed equally at making such contacts, there is not likely to be a problem. But if one is significantly less active in making friends, some resentment may build up. (*passive*)

6. Straight talk about this situation in orientation sessions is very important. Shy freshmen who are prepared for it and see it as bound to happen are less likely to take it personally if it happens to them. (*inevitability*)

7. Those freshmen who are more socially successful can help a roommate who is experiencing things differently. (*the converse*)

8. Of course, no student has an obligation to make sure that his or her roommate has a good time. By college, young people are presumed to have developed some social skills of their own. (*guarantee,* noun)

Word Form Chart			
Noun	Verb	Adjective	Adverb
deviation deviant	deviate	deviant	....

E. Write the answers to the questions in your notebook, using the form of *deviate* in parentheses. Refer to Reading 1 for information. Compare sentences with a partner.

1. Why are many college freshmen worried about rooming with a stranger? (*deviate*)

2. Is it abnormal behavior for someone to tell lies in a MySpace profile? (*deviant,* adjective)

3. Would it be typical for a college to allow freshmen to choose their own roommates? (*deviation*)

4. What do you think would happen if, after checking a social-networking site, a student thought a prospective roommate was dangerously abnormal? (*deviant,* noun)

5. Why did Brandi get upset after first seeing Sarah's profile? (*deviate*)

BEFORE YOU READ

Read these questions. Discuss your answers in a small group.

1. Within the student body at your school (or at a school you used to attend), are there smaller social groups? Do they have names? What brings these groups together?

2. Do you belong to any social groups at your school (or at a school you used to attend)? Are these formal groups or just informal collections of friends?

3. Have you ever known anyone who seemed totally out of place at school, who had only a few friends or none at all? Describe that person. Why do you think that person was so out of place?

READING STRATEGY

After reading this article, answer these questions in a paragraph about 75 words long:

What social groups are there at Chaparral High School? What determines the social groups students are in?

As you read, highlight and annotate the information you think will be valuable in your answer.

READ

This case study examines the social groups at a high school in Arizona.

High School Society: Who Belongs Where?

Look around the sprawling Chaparral High School campus in Scottsdale, Arizona, at lunch time, and the social geography of the 1,850 students is clearly instituted. The football
5 players and their friends have the center table outdoors. In back of them, other popular students chat cheerfully—an attractive array of cheerleaders, lesser jocks[1], and members of the student government. If you qualify for
10 membership under some unwritten clause in the group's unwritten rulebook—even if no one has ever met you before—you've got it made. Lauren, a sophomore cheerleader, notes that "unqualified" students would never dare sit
15 where she's sitting. "But once you're in with the girls, everyone is really friendly to you. When I made cheerleader, it was like I was just set."

Inside, in the cafeteria, a converse society exists. There are more braces[2] and glasses and
20 hair that doesn't quite have a shape. These are the skateboarders, the so-called nerds[3], those who say they are just regular, the freshmen who have not yet found their place. They may have lower social status than the sunny groups
25 outside, but they generally feel they have, or

---

[1] *jock*: an athlete; someone whose main interest is sports
[2] *braces*: teeth-straightening equipment applied directly onto the teeth
[3] *nerd*: someone whose main interest is academics, especially math or science, and who is unconcerned about popular styles and activities

eventually will have, a social place they can live with. There are many other lunchtime domains as well. A bunch of art students eat in the studios, and some band members gather by the music building. Dozens of drama students eat in the theater building, where they are joined by some students whose looks or manners deviate from the norm but who find the theater group more tolerant than most.

Despite all the choices, a few students still have no clique. They eat upstairs or alone outside the library, or they just passively wander, their heads low as they pass clumps of noisy schoolmates. They are blank-faced reminders that a public high school has to admit all kinds of students, but it cannot guarantee them all a place.

Chaparral is a large, well-regarded high school in an affluent suburb. It is a pleasant place, where parents, teachers, and students take justifiable pride in their facilities, their community, and their achievements. Compared with big-city schools, these schools do not look very diverse. The majority of the students are white, middle class, and dressed in the same handful of brand names. But the reality is far more complex. Those who run such good suburban schools are well aware that horrifying school violence has happened at this kind of place, not at tough inner-city high schools.

They speculate about the reasons for this. The nation's dropout rate has declined sharply since the 1960s, especially in suburban schools. Poor urban schools still lose many of their problem students to the streets. Suburban schools still have them. "It used to be that the kids who were really having trouble, the misfits, would leave," said John Kriekard, the principal at Chaparral. But now, "we serve all kinds of kids and we have to try to be all things to all people."

He and others also emphasize the central role schools play in suburban life. "In big cities, there are lots of places where kids make connections, where they have pieces of their lives," he said. "But in a place like this, we're pretty much it."

[4] *loser*: (slang) a person who is not successful or popular

This maximizes the influence that school society has on a student's overall life. Adolescence has always been a time of identity formation, with inclusion and exclusion, trying out new ideas, styles, and friends. And these are not primarily girl issues. No matter what your gender, good looks, cool friends, academic achievement, and money have always defined the social terrain.

A few troubled students would continually disrupt the whole school unless someone—if not the principal, then the law—intervened. They are likely to be rootless and poorly directed, and their chances of finding effective control at home are slim. Economic factors are less important than family factors and previous social experience. Such behavior is a call for help, not for material goods. To a teenager who has little experience with acceptance and security, these advantages seem to go arbitrarily to some people and not to others, certainly not to them.

Carol Miller Lieber, a former principal, says many students entering high school already see themselves as losers[4]. Not surprisingly, this alters their perception of the entire school. Studies show that students who see themselves inevitably as outside the winners' circle have far more negative views of a school than either the teachers or the most successful students. "In these big high-powered suburban high schools, there's a very dominant winner culture, including the jocks, the advanced-placement kids, the student government and, depending on the school, the drama kids or the service clubs," she said. "The winners are a smaller group than we'd like to think, and high school life is very different for those who experience it as the losers. They become part of the invisible middle and suffer in silence, alienated and without any real connection to any adult." Interviews with Chaparral students confirm the research: the popular students who lunch outside were far more likely than the ones sitting inside to say that they love the school and feel connected to at least one teacher.

Now, write the paragraph assigned on page 106. Use your highlighting and annotation to help you. Read your paragraph to a partner and discuss your ideas.

READING COMPREHENSION

Mark each sentence as *T* (true) or *F* (false) according to the information in Reading 2. Use the dictionary to help you understand new words.

.... **1.** At Chaparral High School, athletes have the highest social position.

.... **2.** Passive students must ask special permission from the school to eat lunch outdoors.

.... **3.** Most students who don't fit in with any clique disrupt the whole school.

.... **4.** Someone who becomes a cheerleader is guaranteed acceptance at that group's lunch table.

.... **5.** Public schools are required to accept even troubled students.

.... **6.** In a suburb, the school is likely to provide most of a student's social experience.

.... **7.** The majority of students in a typical high school see themselves as winners.

.... **8.** Social acceptance in high school leads to positive attitudes toward school.

STEP I VOCABULARY ACTIVITIES: Word Level

A. Complete the sentences about social groups in high school using the target vocabulary in the box. Use each item one time. The synonyms in parentheses can help you.

clause	gender	instituted
deviate	guaranteed	intervene
domain	inevitable	so-called

.... **a.** "When kids are tossed together everyday, six hours a day for the entire school year," says psychologist Thomas J. Berdnt, "friendship groupings are
...."
(impossible to avoid)

.... **b.** At one high school near Chicago, the social groups take their names from the places students like to sit. The .... "wall" people are
(labeled)
fashionable students who hang out at a bench along a wall near the cafeteria. The "trophy-case" kids are students who sit on the floor under a display of sports awards.

.... **c.** These "friendship groupings," better known as cliques, are small, tightly knit groups that establish a social .... for people who share
(territory)
interests or characteristics.

.... **d.** Cliques "can be based on appearance, athletic ability, academic achievement, social or economic status, talent, seeming sophistication," or ability to attract people of the opposite .... , according to adolescent
(sex)
development experts Anita Gurian and Alice Pope.

.... **e.** Members of cliques often share the same values and exhibit the same behavior. Although they have been known to form in elementary school, cliques are more normally .... among middle and high
(established)
school students.

.... **f.** Once inside a group, a student is careful not to .... from any
(go in a different direction)
of the unwritten rules.

.... **g.** Someone with distinctive tastes in clothes, hair style, or music is almost .... to be considered part of a clique of people with similar
(certain)
tastes. This is true whether or not the student socializes with these people.

.... **h.** While every high school seems to have its own "jocks" or "nerds," the local environment at a particular school may .... and create a
(step into the situation)
special set of cliques.

B. Put the sentences in activity A into a logical order to describe high school social groups. (More than one order may be possible.) Read your sequence to a partner.

C. Many academic words are also considered formal words. Which of the target words in this unit (see the chart on page 99) are more formal synonyms for these informal words and phrases? Be sure to use the right forms of the target words.

Informal	Formal
1. by chance	....
2. be different	....
3. get involved	....
4. opposite	....
5. certain	....

D. Read the sample sentences that feature forms of the word *diverse*. Then, answer the questions below in your notebook, using a dictionary as suggested. Compare answers with a partner.

> **a.** *Diversity* of opinion makes our staff meetings very lively.
> **b.** My son's school is culturally *diverse*, so they celebrate 17 or 18 holidays every year.
> **c.** The company decided to *diversify* and make a wide range of products.
> **d.** A *diversified* set of investments will contain some stocks, some bonds, and some real estate.

1. Put a check (✓) next to the word closest in meaning to *diverse*. Consult your dictionary before you answer.

   .... wayward   .... alien   .... variegated   .... complicit

2. Each of the sentences in the box above indicates that something is diverse. What is it?

   a. ....   **c.** ....

   b. ....   **d.** ....

3. Look at the sample sentences in your dictionary for *diverse* and its forms. What is diverse in each of those samples?

4. Does *diverse* have any forms that are not used in the sample sentences in the box above? If so, what are they? Consult your dictionary.

STEP II VOCABULARY ACTIVITIES: Sentence Level

> Most public high schools in the United States allow students a great deal of self-expression. Rules about clothing, hair styles, jewelry, and other fashion items are quite loose. All this freedom can shock visitors from other countries—or even Americans who haven't seen a high school in 15 or 20 years.

E. In each of the situations below, a high school student engages in a kind of self-expression. For each situation, answer these three questions in your notebook:

   a. Is this contrary to normal behavior? How does it deviate from the norm?
   b. Should the school institute a rule against it? Why or why not?
   c. Should the right to do this be guaranteed? Why or why not?

Refer to the readings in this unit and your personal opinions.

1. A boy wears a hat in class.

   ....

   ....

2. A girl and her boyfriend kiss and hug each other in the cafeteria.

   ....

   ....

3. A girl wears white face make-up so thick and heavy it looks like a mask.

....

....

4. A student stands in front of the school and shouts criticism of school policies.

....

....

5. A student wears a T-shirt with an obscene word on it.

....

....

6. A student comes to school unwashed, smelly, and wearing dirty clothes.

....

....

F. Discuss your opinions about the situations in activity E in a small group. Then, prepare an oral report that summarizes your discussion of one of the situations. Present your report to the class.

G. Look at these arguments for and against being part of a clique in high school. Restate each idea in your notebook, using some form of the word in parentheses. Then, write a paragraph that expresses your own opinion. Try to use as many target words as possible in your work. Be prepared to read your paragraph or debate this issue in class.

For	Against
Students are able to better develop their special skills if they spend time with people who share their interests. For example, a student interested in literature needs to be around others who can discuss books and present opposing viewpoints. (*converse*)	By hanging out in groups of students much like themselves, students develop a narrow perspective. High school should be a time for exploring life's possibilities, not for restricting yourself. (*maximize*)
During the teen years, students need the security of a group of friends. They are moving away from the protected environment of home and need a safe, comfortable refuge. (*guarantee*)	Blending in too much with others discourages students from being individuals. Teenagers who could be leaders fail to step up, preferring not to call attention to themselves. (*passive*)
You cannot stop students from forming social groups. Rather than wasting time trying to tell students who they can socialize with, parents and the school should give these groups constructive things to do. (*inevitable*)	Teenagers appreciate the guidance of adults when it comes to choosing friends. When adults assert their experience, teens may act annoyed. In the long run, however, they will appreciate the help adults give. (*intervene*)

H. Self-Assessment Review: Go back to page 99 and reassess your knowledge of the target vocabulary. How has your understanding of the words changed? What words do you feel most comfortable with now?

WRITING AND DISCUSSION TOPICS

1. High school groups often form around common interests like music. What other interests unite students into a social group? What types of activities do these cliques enjoy?

2. As Reading 1 suggests, young people increasingly use the Internet to interact with other people. Describe some ways this is done. If you often communicate via the Internet, use some of your own experiences as examples.

3. The social groups in high school are portrayed in many movies. Watch all or part of a movie that you know that shows high school cliques and write a short report about it. Does the clique have a name? Who belongs to it? What makes them different from other students? How do the members treat students outside the group?

4. Psychologists point out that, to a teenager, the opinions of friends are often more influential than the opinions of parents. Therefore, it is important for teenagers to choose their friends carefully. Do your friends influence you more strongly than your parents do? Why or why not? Are there things you can learn from friends that you cannot learn from parents? Explain.

5. If parents feel that their child's clique is having too great an effect on him or her, should they intervene? Why or why not? What should they do?

TRUE AND FALSE

In this unit, you will

- read about factual accuracy in news stories and "reality" in news photographs.
- learn about context clues for a sequence.
- increase your understanding of the target academic words for this unit:

amend	eliminate	grant	levy	restrict
apparent	emphasis	ignorance	perceive	submit
assign	ethic	insert	purchase	successor

SELF-ASSESSMENT OF TARGET WORDS

Think carefully about how well you know each target word in this unit. Then, write it in the appropriate column in the chart.

I have never seen the word before.	I have seen the word but am not sure what it means.	I understand the word when I see or hear it in a sentence.	I have tried to use the word, but I am not sure I am using it correctly.	I use the word with confidence in either speaking *or* writing.	I use the word with confidence, both in speaking *and* writing.

MORE WORDS YOU'LL NEED

editor: a person who is in charge of a newspaper or part of a newspaper

journalism: the profession of collecting, writing, and publishing news

account: a report or description of something that has happened

rumor: a piece of information or a story that people talk about, but that may not be true

BEFORE YOU READ

Read these questions. Discuss your answers in a small group.

1. Have you ever known anyone who was the victim of an untrue rumor? Was the person harmed in any way? What happened?

2. How do news organizations gather information for their reports? What problems might they encounter when gathering it?

3. Do you think most of the news reports you receive are true? Why or why not? How can you know for sure whether they are true?

READ

This article discusses the dangers of inaccurate information in news reports.

A Game of Checkers

It was all a mistake, but that was no comfort to the Vorick family of southern California. On a cable television channel in 2005, a news commentator said that the owner of a grocery
5 store in the Los Angeles area was a terrorist and that he lived at a certain address in the town of La Habra. The address belonged to the Voricks. Day and night, people drove by their house and shouted rude comments. Someone,
10 **apparently** not the best speller in town, spray-painted "Terrist" on their property. Their sense of privacy disappeared as strangers drove up, photographed the house, and drove silently away.

15 The commentator should have checked his facts before he spoke. The supposed "terrorist" had once lived at that address, but that was before the Voricks bought it three years earlier. And another small thing: The man had never
20 been charged with terrorism or any other crime. The cable network had a lot of apologizing to do.

Mistakes will happen, but the errors in this case were easily preventable. Any college
25 journalism student would have known what to do—a simple Internet search of property

ownership in La Habra and a quick check to see if the "terrorist" had a police record. **Inserting** this one priceless step in the process
30 might have taken the staff 30 minutes or so. Carelessly bypassing it was very costly, both for the commentator (who lost his job) and the cable network. Many advertisers are nervous about **purchasing** air time on a network that is
35 **perceived** as careless. If either the Voricks or the alleged[1] terrorist decides to file a lawsuit, the court could **levy** huge penalties against the cable network, the commentator, or both.

Reluctant to expose themselves to such
40 penalties, most magazines, television stations, and other media outlets employ fact-checkers or "researchers" of some type. They are usually young, relatively inexperienced members of the editorial staff. When a report, script, article, or
45 manuscript is being prepared, the fact-checkers are **assigned** to make sure everything is right. They check the spelling of names, the accuracy of numbers, the sequence of events, and the sources of quotations. Their tools are Internet
50 search engines, dictionaries, history books, telephones, and public records of every sort. No questionable item can be **ignored**. If they don't know whether something is correct, they have to find out.

[1] *alleged*: accused but not proven

Most journalists believe they have an **ethical** responsibility to be as accurate as possible. Sometimes that involves fact-checking, but sometimes it cannot. Daily newspapers do not generally employ separate fact-checkers.
60 Reporters are expected to get the facts right in the copy[2] they **submit**. A copy editor[3] might occasionally question a "fact" that seems incorrect, but newspapers operate under severe time restrictions. Re-checking most information
65 is usually not possible.

For media that have less pressing deadlines, the story is different. Some magazine fact-checking departments are legendary for their thoroughness. *The New Yorker* magazine of the
70 mid-20th century had a reputation for fact-checking excellence. Then things declined a bit in the 1970s and 1980s. In the 1990s, managing editor Tina Brown, **emphasizing** accuracy, hired the people necessary to restore the department's
75 glory. According to one rumor, there was an article that mentioned a singer had gestured with both arms. An eager fact-checker asked the singer whether he, in fact, has two arms. Even other publications **granted** that *The New*
80 *Yorker* was the fact-checking champion. Jobs in the fact-checking department at the magazine became a desirable stepping-stone to high-level editorial jobs.

In far more cases, fact-checking departments
85 have been severely cut back or even **eliminated**. When that happens, the few checkers who remain cannot afford to spend much time on any one issue. As a result, some stories have slipped through the system, though they probably
90 should have been dropped. One account in *Newsweek* in 2005, about the behavior of U.S. soldiers, sparked religious riots that killed at least 15 people. Because the story had never been fact-checked, *Newsweek's* editors could
95 not show evidence that it was true. It was based on statements by only one source, and no one else could verify[4] it. Eventually the magazine retracted[5] the story, an indication that it was probably not true. Of course, by that time the
100 damage had been done.

Good fact-checking early in a story's life is vital. Any errors must be **amended** right from the start. Once one magazine or television station has reported a story, others will soon do
105 the same. Consequently, mistakes get passed on and circulated widely. Even if they are eventually discovered, they are very hard to remove from the realm of what "everybody knows."

---

[2] *copy*: written material intended to be printed in a newspaper
[3] *copy editor*: a person whose job is to correct and prepare text for printing
[4] *verify*: confirm
[5] *retract*: say that something printed earlier should not have been printed

READING COMPREHENSION

Mark each sentence as *T* (true) or *F* (false) according to the information in Reading 1. Use the dictionary to help you understand new words.

.... **1.** A convicted terrorist once lived in the house that the Voricks purchased.

.... **2.** The TV commentator who mentioned the Voricks' address lost his job.

.... **3.** People distrust organizations that spread incorrect information.

.... **4.** Most fact-checkers have a lot of experience in specialized fields.

continued

.... **5.** If a checker does not know whether a fact in a story is correct, he or she has an ethical duty to assign the story to another fact-checker.

.... **6.** During the 1990s, *The New Yorker* had a very good fact-checking department.

.... **7.** A clever fact-checker discovered that a singer mentioned in an article had lost an arm.

.... **8.** *Newsweek* made a mistake by basing a story on statements that could not be checked.

.... **9.** Some incorrect news stories have led to injury or death.

.... **10.** An incorrect "fact" is likely to be repeated by other news outlets.

READING STRATEGY: Understanding Sequences

Articles often contain sequences of events. Sequences are important to understand because they help the reader understand how things and ideas relate to each other. Sequences are marked by several different types of signals:

- Time expressions: *in 2005, at the end of February, last week*
- Adverbs of sequence: *first, then, afterward*
- Verb tenses: past, present perfect, past perfect

Use the sequence signals in Reading 1 to complete these sequences in the proper time order.

The Voricks

a. *The alleged "terrorist" lives in the house the Voricks would buy.*

b.

c.

d.

The New Yorker

a.

b.

c. *Tina Brown becomes managing editor.*

d.

The *Newsweek* story

a.

b.

c.

d.

e. *Newsweek retracts the story.*

STEP I VOCABULARY ACTIVITIES: Word Level

A. Read these excerpts from another article about a mistake on a television news show. For each item, cross out the one word or phrase in parentheses with a different meaning from the other three choices. Compare answers with a partner.

1. Imagine this scenario: You go to a television station for a job interview. Someone walks into a room and (*seemingly / clearly / apparently / evidently*) calls your name. You follow.

2. The next thing you know, you're being interviewed on live television regarding an event you are totally (*expert / uninformed / ignorant / clueless*) about.

3. You start to see it might be a mistake, especially when you realize the name the interviewer calls you isn't actually yours. It's close, but not quite. The interviewer doesn't seem to (*notice / perceive / admit / see*) that anything is wrong.

4. You answer her questions (*hesitantly / reluctantly / unethically / unwillingly*) with general statements. Still, she keeps interviewing you.

5. This is what happened on a recent live news show aired by the British Broadcasting Corporation (BBC). Even the man who was supposed to be interviewed—but wasn't—(*admits / grants / concedes / hopes*) that it was pretty funny.

6. The producer who called out for the guest in the waiting room should probably have (*emphasized / stressed / amended / highlighted*) the last name. The intended guest is a British commentator on Internet issues named "Guy." The man actually led into the studio is a computer expert, also named "Guy."

7. The wrong Guy probably (*submitted to / showed up for / put up with / tolerated*) the surprise question session because he thought it was some new kind of job interview.

8. The BBC apologized for the mistake, but they did not publicly (*assign / apply / accept / attribute*) blame for it.

B. Match these expressions that use the word *grant* with their definitions. Compare answers with a partner.

.... 1. grant permission   **a.** give a prize

.... 2. student grant   **b.** give someone what he or she asks for

.... 3. grant admission   **c.** "Of course, . . ."

.... 4. grant an award   **d.** allow something to happen

.... 5. take something for granted   **e.** money given to enable education

.... 6. research grant   **f.** money given to enable scientific study

.... 7. "Granted, . . ."   **g.** allow someone entry to a restricted area or organization

.... 8. grant a wish   **h.** assume that something is true without confirming it

The word *perceive* has two meanings. It can mean "to become aware of something through the senses," usually through seeing or observation. It can also mean "to see or think of something in a particular way." Two people can see the same thing but perceive it quite differently. The noun form for both meanings is *perception*.

C. Which of these things can humans perceive? Put a check (✓) next to them. For each item that you check, explain to a partner different ways it might be perceived by different people.

.... 1. the crying of a baby

.... 2. a person's age

.... 3. the age of planet Earth

.... 4. someone else's emotions (fear, joy, etc.)

.... 5. a possible solution to a problem

.... 6. the colors of a rainbow

.... 7. electricity

.... 8. infection by a bacterium or virus

STEP II VOCABULARY ACTIVITIES: Sentence Level

The words *ignore* and *be ignorant of* have the same roots but very different meanings.

ignore   pay no attention to someone or something

be ignorant of   not know about something

The noun *ignorance* and the adjective *ignorant* both refer to the second meaning.

D. Rephrase these statements using the form of *ignore* that is right for the context. Compare sentences with a partner.

1. The driver was in a hurry and decided not to follow the speed limit.

   ....

2. The driver said he didn't know the speed limit had changed, but still got a ticket for speeding.

   ....

3. The police officer told him that not knowing the law is no excuse for breaking the law.

   ....

4. While the reporter was in Malawi she embarrassed herself several times because she wasn't familiar with the local customs.

   ....

5. The editor dropped the story because she felt the reporter had purposefully left out information that didn't support his point of view.

   ....

6. The editor told him that pretending not to notice a problem will not make it go away.

   ....

Word Form Chart

Noun	Verb	Adjective	Adverb
....	....	apparent	apparently
assignment	assign	assigned	....
grant	grant	....	for granted
submission	submit	submissive	submissively
successor succession	succeed	successive	successively

E. Read another account related to accuracy in journalism. Then, in your notebook, restate the sentences, using the words in parentheses. Concentrate on main ideas and leave out details. Be prepared to read aloud or discuss your work in class.

1. In 1981, a reporter for the *Washington Post* newspaper turned in a story, titled "Jimmy's World," about an 8-year-old drug addict living in the nation's capital. (*submit*)

2. The sad story created a stir, and the reporter, Janet Cooke, became a kind of media superstar. A few months later, she was given a Pulitzer Prize, the highest award in American journalism, for her work on the story. (*granted*)

3. Meanwhile, Washington's mayor, Marion Barry, launched a huge effort, involving dozens of city employees, to find Jimmy. (*assign*)

4. Soon, it became clear to city officials that the boy probably did not exist. (*apparent*)

5. One investigation after another found problems not only with the story but also with Cooke's statements about her education and previous experience. (*successive*)

6. A few days after the prize was awarded, however, the *Post* confirmed that the story was a fake and issued an apology to its readers. (*submit*)

7. Cooke resigned from the Post and gave back her prize. She laid the blame for the problem on her editors, who, she claims, put unbearable pressure on her to produce a big story. (*assign*)

8. At the *Post*, publisher Dan Graham—who had inherited his powerful position from his legendary mother, Katherine Graham—set up measures to better check the credentials of reporters it plans to hire. (*successor*)

BEFORE YOU READ

Read these questions. Discuss your answers in a small group.

1. There is a saying, "The camera doesn't lie." Do you think this is true? Why or why not?

2. Have you ever taken a picture that was not as good as you had hoped? What was wrong with it? Could you do anything to fix it?

3. You have probably seen pictures supposedly showing UFOs, the Loch Ness monster, the Yeti, or other controversial phenomena. Do you find the pictures convincing? Why or why not?

READ

This editorial examines the practice of using computer programs to "fix up" news photographs.

Playing with the Pixels

1   A freelance photographer working in Beirut, Lebanon, tried a little too hard to convey the horror of war. He altered at least two photographs he took there during the summer of 2006. In one, he used computer software to darken and thicken smoke rising from bombed buildings. In another he inserted objects below and behind an F-16 fighter jet to make it look like the jet was firing multiple missiles. In reality, the jet was firing no missiles at all, only a flare. He then submitted both pictures to a news service, which purchased them and sent them out for newspapers to use.

2   Unfortunately for the photographer, his alterations were soon apparent to some sharp-eyed readers. Many Internet bloggers pointed out clues—buildings that appeared twice in the same picture, inconsistent shadows, identical vapor trails behind the "missiles." Within hours, the news service stopped distributing the pictures, and dismissed the photographer. Subsequently, they issued a statement that such fakery[1] was unethical and had no place in the news business.

[1] *fakery*: falseness

3   Maybe so, but it happens regularly. Recently, another news service got caught sending out an altered photo of an Alaskan pipeline worker. A newspaper in North Carolina fired a photographer for changing the color of the sky in a picture of firefighters. In 2003, a California newspaper fired a photographer for combining two pictures from Iraq, taken moments apart, into one. In 2004, the re-election campaign for President George W. Bush reluctantly admitted altering a video by inserting faces into a crowd of soldiers listening to Bush. You could tell because some faces appeared at several places in the crowd at the same time. Some of these episodes were quite serious attempts to mislead the public, and some were relatively trivial[2]. All of them undermine the public's trust in the reality of news photographs.

4   Actually, that's good. The public tends to assign too much "reality" to what they see in photographs anyway. We should approach all news photos as somewhat unreal.

5   What does it mean for a photograph to be true? That it captures what we would perceive if we were standing where the camera was? That's nonsense. A camera sees quite differently from

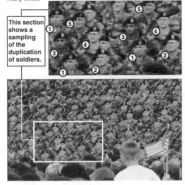

Bush campaign digitally altered TV ad

President Bush's campaign acknowledged Thursday that it had digitally altered a photo that appeared in a national cable television commercial. In the photo, a handful of soldiers were multiplied many times.

This section shows a sampling of the duplication of soldiers.

a human eye. "Normal" human vision is roughly equivalent to what you get from a 35 millimeter camera lens zoomed out a little bit—to between 42 mm and 50 mm. A lens longer than that shows details no human eye could see. A lens shorter than that shows an unnaturally broad view and too little detail.

6   There are restrictions to the way any camera can capture an image. Details that you or I could easily see in person may be lost in glare or sunk in a dark spot. Is it okay, then, to use photo-editing software to emphasize such details and amend the "inaccurate" picture? Doing this would, in some ways, make the photo more accurate. What about emphasizing lost details that would *not* be visible to an eyewitness? That would make the photo more accurate in other ways. Should news organizations grant their photographers permission to do that? If not, then should we ban photos taken through microscopes? You can see how quickly the situation gets confused.

7   Of course, photographers "alter" every photograph they take, simply because they have to make choices about how to take it. They have to decide where to stand, how to stand, whether to put a filter on the lens, and so on. Editors alter them as well, literally and figuratively. Long before digital photography came along, newspaper editors chopped the edges off photographs, enlarged them, and eliminated scratches or spots with correction fluid. Photo-editing software is simply a far smarter **successor** to those tools. Editors also write headlines and captions, words that can dramatically affect the viewer's perception of the image. A picture of a fallen tree is just a fallen tree—until words tell you whether it's a good thing (Land Cleared for New Hospital) or a bad thing (Storm Downs 200-Year-Old Oak). What you see when you contemplate a news photo is what you're told to see.

8   Sometimes perception is controlled by what you're allowed to see. When Ronald Reagan visited Germany's Bitburg cemetery in 1985, presidential aides levied strict limitations on photographers. They could shoot only from certain vantage points. From these sites, they could not get both the president and the graves of Nazi soldiers in the same shot. The pictures that came out of that event certainly weren't fake, but were they really true? President Franklin Delano Roosevelt (in office 1933–1945), who had a disease called polio, used a wheelchair every day throughout his presidency. Yet no major American newspaper or magazine published a picture of him in a wheelchair through that entire 12-year period. The editors of these publications were not ignorant of the president's disability. The White House did not keep photographers away. The editors simply didn't want the public to get the impression that their president was too weak to govern. Looked at as a whole, was the photographic record of FDR's presidency true?

9   Needless to say, news photographers shouldn't doctor photographs any more than reporters should make up quotes. But "doctoring" is a slippery concept, and photographic truth is an illusion.

---

[2] *trivial*: of little importance

READING COMPREHENSION

Mark each sentence as *T* (true) or *F* (false) according to the information in **Reading 2**. Use the dictionary to help you understand new words.

.... **1.** The photographer in Lebanon apparently did not add anything by altering his photos.

.... **2.** The news service submitted a public apology for sending out the altered photos from Lebanon.

.... **3.** A presidential campaign once released a video altered to eliminate some people who were at an event.

.... **4.** Sometimes, altering a photo has no truly serious consequences.

.... **5.** A photographer alters a photograph simply by deciding how to take it.

.... **6.** The best definition of a "true" photograph is that it shows what someone on the scene would see with his or her eyes.

.... **7.** Photo-editing software can emphasize light or shadow.

.... **8.** Photos taken through a microscope are not actually photos at all.

.... **9.** Franklin Roosevelt was photographed with his wheelchair, but leading newspapers were reluctant to publish the pictures.

.... **10.** It is a mistake to believe that photographs tell the truth.

READING STRATEGY

A. What sequence is described in paragraphs 1 and 2 of Reading 2? List at least six events in that sequence, in order.

Event

....

....

....

....

....

....

B. In your notebook, write a short paragraph in which you put the events from paragraph 8 of Reading 2 into chronological order. Use at least five events and include signals.

STEP I VOCABULARY ACTIVITIES: Word Level

A. Complete the sentences about nature photography by using the target vocabulary in the box. Use each item one time. The synonyms in parentheses can help you.

amend	emphasize	perceived
an apparently	ignores	restrict
eliminated	inserted	successor

.... **a.** Ansel Adams, a master of American landscape photography, blacked out inconvenient elements from his photographs. Artistic considerations demanded that he .... some things and play down others.
(stress)

.... **b.** Eliot Porter was a pioneer in using color in nature shots. He hated dishonest photos but showed no reluctance to .... nature as necessary.
(alter) He once cut a cactus to pieces to get a shot of a roadrunner's nest.

.... **c.** In 1982, National Geographic put a digitally altered photo of Egypt's Pyramids of Giza on one of its covers. Ever since, there have been calls to .... the use of computers to alter travel and nature photos.
(limit)

.... **d.** No one wants to be .... as favoring fake photos. In 1991, the
(viewed) National Press Photographers Association (NPPA) came out against digital manipulation.

.... **e.** Manipulation with photo-editing software is simply the ....
(follow-up) to earlier darkroom techniques used by history's best nature photographers.

.... **f.** It is .... reasonable policy, but it .... some
(a seemingly) *(does not pay attention to)* practices that are common among nature photographers.

.... **g.** The great Paul Strand was also very much opposed to doctoring photos, but even he drew in manhole covers or .... people from photos
(took out) to make shots look better.

.... **h.** The NPPA .... this sentence into an official policy
(added) statement: "As journalists we believe the guiding principle of our profession is accuracy; therefore, we believe it is wrong to alter the content of a photograph in any way that deceives the public."

B. Put the sentences in activity A into a logical sequence. (More than one order may be possible.) Read your sequence to a partner.

C. Many academic words are also considered formal words. Which of the target words in this unit (see the chart on page 113) are more formal synonyms for these informal words and phrases? Be sure to use the right forms of the target words.

Informal	Formal
1. buy	....
2. to get rid of	....
3. give	....
4. notice	....
5. hand in	....
6. change	....

D. Read the sample sentences that feature forms of the word *submit*. Then, answer the questions below in your notebook, using a dictionary as suggested. Compare answers with a partner.

> a. *Submit* your application and a copy of your resume to the Human Resources Department.
> b. None of my *submissions* to the magazine has ever been accepted.
> c. A dog will indicate *submission* to the pack leader by putting its ears back and tucking its tail between its legs.
> d. Even the president has to *submit* to the law.

1. The word *submit* has two main meanings. Put a check (✓) next to the word most similar to each meaning. Consult your dictionary before you answer.

   Meaning 1: .... apply .... withdraw .... satisfy .... offer

   Meaning 2: .... defer .... resist .... supply .... suffer

2. Which sample sentences in the box above go with each meaning?

   Meaning 1: ....

   Meaning 2: ....

3. Look at the sample sentences in your dictionary for *submit* and its forms.

   For meaning 1, what is being submitted?

   ....

   For meaning 2, what is being submitted to?

   ....

4. Does *submit* have any forms that are not used in the sample sentences in the box above? If so, what are they? Consult your dictionary.

STEP II VOCABULARY ACTIVITIES: Sentence Level

Editors make changes to most news stories their reporters submit. Some of these are small changes like punctuation, grammar, or spelling. Others affect the content of a story. These changes could be made for several reasons:

- Some information in the original is inaccurate.
- The editor is worried that something in the story will cause the paper to be sued or will offend people.
- The editor or owner doesn't like a story's thesis or point of view.

They might also assign a story and tell a reporter what point of view to take.

E. Each of these situations involves a decision, by an editor or some other manager, that some people perceive as unethical. For each situation, answer these questions:

a. What apparent reasons were there for the action?

b. How did the emphasis of the story change?

c. Was the decision justified? Why or why not?

Refer to the readings in this unit and your personal opinions.

1. A reporter submitted a negative review of a restaurant that advertised frequently in his newspaper. The editor rejected it. He had a positive review written and published it instead.

   ....

   ....

   ....

2. The sheriff's office asked the town's newspaper to insert a false story about a house fire and the paper agreed. The fake story was used to catch a suspect who had offered to pay someone to set the fire. The story was the "proof" that the fire happened. The suspect paid the person, which confirmed the suspect's guilt.

   ....

   ....

   ....

3. A high government official changed parts of a report on global warming. The report emphasized that the Earth's climate is heating up. The official eliminated that language and made it seem that this apparent warming only may be happening.

   ....

   ....

   ....

F. Discuss your opinions about the situations in activity E in a small group. Then, prepare an oral report that summarizes your discussion of one of the situations. Present your report to the class.

G. Look at these arguments for and against the digital alteration of news photographs. Restate each idea in your notebook, using some form of the word(s) in parentheses. Then, write a paragraph that expresses your own opinion. Try to use as many target words as possible in your work. Be prepared to read your paragraph or debate this issue in class.

For	Against
If a photographer sees that a photograph fails to communicate what was actually happening, he or she has an obligation to fix it. Cameras can distort reality. (*emphasis / eliminate*)	A photograph should speak for itself. Viewers who see the photograph differently from the photographer may be able to sense things the photographer missed. (*perceive*)
Unlike earlier methods of repairing negatives, digital alterations do not ruin the original photo. People concerned about accuracy can compare altered and unaltered versions. (*restrict*)	Although several versions of a digital photo can coexist, the only one that matters is the one that is published. The first shot placed before the public creates a lasting impression. (*submit*)
No one wants to forbid the use of flashes or special lenses, but people feel free to tell a photographer how to use a computer. (*reluctance*)	Photo software can do things never imagined for other methods of photo manipulation, like adding and deleting things in the image. (*insert / eliminate*)

H. Self-Assessment Review: Go back to page 113 and reassess your knowledge of the target vocabulary. How has your understanding of the words changed? What words do you feel most comfortable with now?

WRITING AND DISCUSSION TOPICS

1. Fashion magazines have sometimes digitally edited photos of models to make them look thinner. This is meant to make designer clothes look better on them. In your opinion, is this a good practice? Explain your point of view.

2. The essayist Susan Sontag once wrote, "In America, the photographer is not simply the person who records the past, but the one who invents it." What do you think this statement means? Do you agree with it?

3. Most newspapers and magazines include a section where they apologize for mistakes they have made in earlier issues. Such a retraction might say something like, "We apologize for incorrectly reporting Mr. Jones's occupation as 'duck driver.' He is a truck driver." If a newspaper printed incorrect information about you, would such an apology be enough to make you feel better? Should the newspaper do anything else to make up for the error? Would you be willing to sue the newspaper in court?

4. Some news organizations openly slant their reports toward one perception or another. They purposefully emphasize one side of a story or ignore aspects of it that do not fit in with their ideas. Some people say that these organizations should not be called "news organizations." They feel that real news is, or should try to be, unbiased and fair. What do you think?

BITES AND STINGS

In this unit, you will

- read about the health effects of being bitten or stung by certain insects or spiders.
- recognize a process structure in a text.
- use a flow chart in your notes to record a process.
- increase your understanding of the target academic words for this unit:

append	contact	initiate	percent	summary
chemical	estimate	minimal	regime	virtual
circumstance	external	neutral	sufficient	

SELF-ASSESSMENT OF TARGET WORDS

Think carefully about how well you know each target word for this unit. Then, write it in the appropriate column in the chart.

I have never seen the word before.	I have seen the word but am not sure what it means.	I understand the word when I see or hear it in a sentence.	I have tried to use the word, but I am not sure I am using it correctly.	I use the word with confidence in either speaking *or* writing.	I use the word with confidence, both in speaking *and* writing.

MORE WORDS YOU'LL NEED

diagnosis: a doctor's final opinion about what illness a person has

therapy: treatment to help cure an illness or injury

tissue: bodily material; there is bone tissue, muscle tissue, nerve tissue, etc.

venom: poison produced in an animal's body for self-defense or to kill prey

BEFORE YOU READ

Read these questions. Discuss your answers in a small group.

1. What kinds of ants are you familiar with? Where do they live? How do they come into contact with humans?

2. Have you ever been stung by an ant, bee, or wasp? How did it feel? What did you do to reduce the pain? How long did its effects last?

3. Name some animals that produce a poison to help protect them against enemies. How strong is their venom? Is it harmful to humans? How does the animal get its venom into the enemy's body?

READ

This excerpt is from a book on insects in everyday life. It discusses a type of insect that is a growing threat in the United States.

Attack of the Fire Ants

The red fire ant, *Solenopsis invicta,* is one of over eighty thousand species of ants worldwide. Like their close relatives, the bees, many species of ant have a sharp **appendage**, called a stinger,
5 at the end of their body. Most bees can sting only once, and then they die. An ant's stinger can be used repeatedly.

A red fire ant

The red fire ant is not native to North America. It arrived on ships from South
10 America in the 1930s through the port of Mobile, Alabama. That landing in Alabama **initiated** a full-scale invasion. Since then, fire ants have spread throughout the southern United States and Puerto Rico.

15 Following World War II, **circumstances** worked in the ants' favor. The fire ant is known as a "tramp" or "weed" species because it thrives (like a weed) in recently cleared or disturbed areas. After the war, there was rapid population
20 growth in the "Sunbelt" of America's south and southwest. Land cleared for new homes, parks, and factories was a perfect habitat for fire ants. By 1950, they had made it halfway up the border between Mississippi and Alabama. Since then,
25 they have become firmly established in Texas, and they are relatively common in Arizona. A few have shown up in California. They may eventually move into some milder parts of Oregon and Washington.

30 Public health experts **estimate** that, in any given year, from 30 to 60 **percent** of people living in fire-ant zones in the United States are stung. The ant grasps the skin with its tiny, powerful jaws, arches its body, injects the
35 stinger into the skin, and releases venom. If not stopped, the ant will rotate itself around and create a whole circle of stings. There's an immediate burning sensation, followed by hours to days of intense itching. **Virtually** everyone
40 who is stung by a fire ant develops a red welt that stays painful for several days. Up to half of the

victims will experience larger reactions near the location of the bite.

Fire ant venom may be toxic to the nervous system. One tree trimmer in Florida suffered serious fire ant attacks three times within one year. After the third attack, his right hand and forearm became numb[1] and his wrist became weak. This condition lasted for about a month. The venom is also *necrotic*—it kills the tissue that it comes in **contact** with. If this necrosis, or tissue death, happens after a sting, permanent scars may remain on a victim's skin. Terrible sores can result if an infection takes hold near the necrotic tissue. The most dangerous physical response to a fire ant sting, however, is an anaphylactic reaction. This is the same kind of reaction some people have to bee stings and is similar to an extreme allergy. It begins with weakness, itching, chest tightness, and wheezing[2]. This can bring on a sharp fall in blood pressure and sometimes even death. In some fire-ant zones, fire ant venom causes more fatal reactions than bee stings. In sensitive people, a single sting is usually enough to initiate the reaction.

Fire ant venom is a watery solution of toxin that affects human mast cells. These cells are filled with a **chemical** called *histamine*. Histamine is the same chemical that triggers the sneezing, itching, and other symptoms of an allergy. When an allergy-causing substance enters the body, the walls of the mast cell weaken until they can no longer contain the histamine. The cell explodes, releasing a rush of histamine. If these histamine explosions occur in the lungs, the reaction can be serious—perhaps including a blockage of the passages that deliver air to the lungs. These lung problems are not common, but they are a real threat to anyone extremely sensitive to fire-ant venom.

[1] *numb*: not able to feel anything
[2] *wheezing*: difficult, noisy breathing

Nothing can completely **neutralize** the effects of fire-ant venom, but people sensitive to it who live in fire-ant territory have some treatment choices. Immunotherapy is currently the best option for **minimalizing** reactions. It consists of a series of injections, administered according to a regular schedule. Initially, patients receive very small amounts of fire-ant venom that their bodies can tolerate. With each injection, the amount of venom is increased, which causes the person's body to start building up resistance to it. Eventually, patients have **sufficient** defenses to tolerate a fire-ant sting. The immunotherapy **regime** is expensive, and it also requires a long-term commitment. Doctors estimate that treatments will take as long as two years.

Fire ant populations have not yet established themselves very far north. Many, many studies have tried to discover which temperatures are too cold for them. In **summary**, research shows that, like any insect, a fire ant becomes less active as the weather grows colder. Eventually, it becomes totally motionless. Fire ants hit this temperature boundary at about 50° Fahrenheit (10° Celsius). Above that temperature, ants are active. Below it, the ants slow down dramatically.

In places where temperatures stay at least this low for much of the year, ant colonies cannot survive outdoors. Right now, this keeps the fire ants from attacking areas east of the Pacific Coast mountain ranges and north of the Ohio River. Some health officials worry that global warming may open the door for the ant armies to march farther north.

A more immediate worry is that ant colonies may take hold inside heated buildings. Under these circumstances, **external** temperatures would make no difference at all and fire ants would become a much bigger problem for humans.

READING COMPREHENSION

Mark each sentence as *T* (true) or *F* (false) according to the information in Reading 1. Use the dictionary to help you understand new words.

.... 1. Red fire ants, like bees, deliver painful bites with their jaws.

.... 2. *Solenopsis invicta* first entered the United States through Puerto Rico.

.... 3. As the population in the U.S. South grew after World War II, more habitats for *Solenopsis* opened up.

.... 4. Very few people living in fire-ant territory ever come into contact with *Solenopsis.*

.... 5. Most people stung by red fire ants do not realize it until several hours later.

.... 6. *Solenopsis* venom can damage nerves and kill cells it touches.

.... 7. Mast cells are external cells on the human body, which fire ants hold onto while they inject venom.

.... 8. There is currently no way to neutralize fire-ant venom.

.... 9. Fire ant populations are unlikely to live where external temperatures go below 50° Fahrenheit much of the year.

.... 10. Environmental circumstances, like global warming, play a part in the spread of the fire-ant population.

READING STRATEGY: Recording Processes with Flow Charts

A process described in a reading may be simple and direct or it could be quite complex. Sometimes, the direction of a process can depend on circumstances. It will take one direction if A happens and another direction if B happens.

A good way to clarify these possibilities in your notes is to use a flow chart. A flow chart shows how one event leads, or flows, into another. It also shows how circumstances might alter the process.

A. Fill in this flow chart that traces the spread of fire ants in the U.S. Refer to Reading 1 for information. Note, the dotted line indicates a future possibility.

fire ants arrive in Mobile, Alabama → ants spread to Mississippi and Alabama → [ ] → ants in California ⤍ mild parts of Oregon and Washington

B. Fill in this flow chart showing what can happen as a result of a fire-ant sting. See Reading 1 for information.

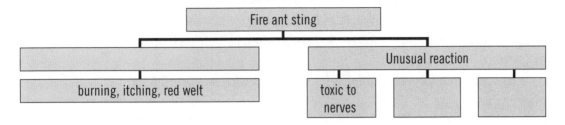

C. In your notebook, create your own flow chart to describe what happens in each "unusual reaction" to a fire-ant sting. See Reading 1 for information. Compare and discuss your flow charts with a partner. Your charts may not be exactly the same.

STEP I VOCABULARY ACTIVITIES: Word Level

A. Read these excerpts from an article on an organic gardening website. The author is giving advice on how to get rid of fire ants without using chemicals. For each excerpt, cross out the one word or phrase in parentheses with a different meaning from the other three choices. Compare answers with a partner.

1. There are several ways to kill a colony of fire ants without using poisonous (*chemicals* / *substances* / *venoms* / *compound*s) that could harm you or the environment.

2. An effective method that requires (*minimal* / *no* / *very little* / *minor*) effort is to "bucket" the colony. After shoveling a mound of ants into a large bucket, simply drown them by mixing soapy water into the sand in the bucket.

3. You could also pour hot water onto the ant mound. Because the water is chemically (*beneficial* / *neutral* / *harmless* / *mild*), it does not damage the soil.

4. Unfortunately, a single treatment with hot water is usually not (*desirable* / *sufficient* / *satisfactory* / *enough*) to kill all the ants in a colony. You'll probably have to repeat the application at least three times.

5. Introducing some (*outside* / *external* / *local* / *exotic*) predator, such as straw mites, can kill ants. Unfortunately, then you have to find a way to get rid of *them*.

6. You probably could kill a colony by pumping exhaust fumes from your car into the mound. I (*estimate* / *argue* / *figure* / *guess*) it would take at least 45 minutes of running your car to begin killing them, instead of just making them unconscious.

7. Remember that household cleaners are chemicals. (*Almost* / *Especially* / *Virtually* / *Practically*) all of them pose a threat to you or your garden. Pouring them on an ant mound is not a good idea.

The word *contact* is similar in meaning to the word *touch*. The verb *contact* is usually used to mean "reach someone for the purpose of communicating."

*They were finally able to **contact** their daughter four days after the storm.*

For less important or less meaningful connections, people often use the verb phrase *come into contact with*.

*She works in a language school, so she **comes into contact with** people from all over the world.*

B. Which of these people or things have you come into contact with? Put a check (✓) next to them. Discuss your experiences with a partner.

.... **1.** the headmaster or principal of your school

.... **2.** a dangerous animal

.... **3.** a celebrity

.... **4.** people from another part of the world

.... **5.** a gangster or dangerous person

.... **6.** something mysterious or hard to explain

.... **7.** serious illness

.... **8.** an extraterrestrial (someone from another planet)

STEP II VOCABULARY ACTIVITIES: Sentence Level

Word Form Chart			
Noun	Verb	Adjective	Adverb
estimate estimation	estimate overestimate underestimate	estimated overestimated underestimated	....

C. Answer these questions in your notebook, using the word in parentheses in your answer. Refer to Reading 1 for information. Compare sentences with a partner.

1. About how many species of ant are there? (*estimate*, verb)

2. About what percentage of the population will get stung in ant territory, according to experts? (*estimated*, adjective)

3. If someone told you that he planned to complete an immunotherapy regime in a month or two, what would you say to him? (*underestimate*)

4. What would you say to a state official who wanted to require everyone in fire-ant territory to get immunotherapy? (*overestimate*)

5. In your opinion, should someone who is sensitive to ant stings live in Arizona? (*estimation*)

Word Form Chart			
Noun	Verb	Adjective	Adverb
circumstance	....	circumstantial	circumstantially
initiation initiative initiator	initiate	....	....
minimalization	minimalize	minimal	minimally
neutralization	neutralize	neutral	....
sufficiency insufficiency	suffice	sufficient insufficient	sufficiently insufficiently

D. Read another account related to insect bites and stings. Then, in your notebook, restate the information using the word in parentheses. Concentrate on main ideas and leave out the less important details. Be prepared to read aloud or discuss your sentences in class.

1. The bites of non-venomous insects can produce many more serious illnesses than the bites of venomous ones. (*initiate*)

2. For one thing, venomous insects account for only a tiny percentage of the insect species on the planet. (*minimal*)

3. Also, the bacteria and other microorganisms carried by insects can do much more damage to a human body than most venoms can. The insect bite itself is not damaging enough to cause a problem. (*sufficiently* or *insufficiently*)

4. In so-called "vector-borne" diseases, like malaria or Lyme disease, the insect is not the dangerous organism but just a carrier—a vector. (*neutral*)

5. About 40 percent of the world's people live in conditions that expose them almost constantly to mosquitoes, including the type that carries malaria. (*circumstance*)

6. Most insect venoms and their effects can be counteracted by simple medicines. This is not the case with vector-borne diseases. (*neutralize*)

7. Governments and nonprofit groups have launched several earnest efforts to reduce the effects of malaria, especially in tropical Africa, Southeast Asia, and Central America. (*initiative*)

8. Although these programs are important and somewhat effective, it is doubtful whether anything humans do could make a big difference in the threat that malaria poses. (*sufficient* or *insufficient*)

BEFORE YOU READ

Read these questions. Discuss your answers in a small group.

1. Think about an incident in which you got insect or spider bites. Where were you when you were bitten? Why do you think the insect or spider bit you? How did you react?

2. In your home town or home region, which insects are a problem? Do they bite? What happens to someone bitten by them?

3. Have you ever been bitten by an insect or spider you did not see? Why didn't you see it?

READ

This article from a popular health magazine focuses on the importance of proper diagnosis and treatment of bites.

You Wouldn't Know It If It Bit You

The young woman had been looking forward to her nice new apartment in Manhattan. Circumstances turned out to be less comfortable than she expected, as this posting
5 to an online forum about insect bites shows.

> I just moved into a newly renovated apartment and got 10 huge, itchy bug bites on my arms, legs, and hip. I thought it was my mattress, so I got rid of it and bought a new one. Still got
> 10 bites and could not find bugs anywhere. I even tried freezing out my apartment by leaving the door open during the winter chill since I heard the bugs can't survive in temps less than 25 degrees. No luck. I went to a dermatologist who
> 15 said the bite pattern isn't like any of the usual apartment pests, and he didn't know what it was. I am miserable. My immune system has reacted to the bites, and I have prickly itching ALL over my body, not just where the bites are, all day
> 20 long. I called my landlord who is sending an exterminator over. Will post to let you know how it goes. If anyone has found the solution, please email me. Thank you!

Throughout North America, countless people
25 crawl into bed at night knowing exactly how the writer feels. Instead of a peaceful night's sleep, they will get a new round of bites by some mysterious pest. Because they don't know what's plaguing them, they have no idea how to
30 stop it. In extreme cases, a concern becomes an obsession. Weakened by a lack of sleep, a victim develops a feeling that biting creatures lurk everywhere. Bites and the fear of them establish a cruel regime, ruling the victim's daytime
35 thoughts and nighttime dreams.

Bites by insects or arachnids—such as fleas, ticks, horseflies, mosquitoes, or bedbugs—are extremely common. Virtually all humans who survive past infancy are bitten at some point in
40 their lives. A bite, which involves a creature's mouth parts, is different from a sting, which is made with a sharp structure appended to a creature's rear end. Most insect bites cause only minimal discomfort, if any at all. The bite
45 might cause a little swelling because chemicals in the bug's saliva[1] irritate the skin. More serious problems are rare. When they do happen, the bite victim's own behavior might be to blame. Your mother summarized it for you when

---

[1] *saliva*: the liquid that is produced in the mouth

you were young: "Don't scratch those bites!" Scratching can open the skin and allow bacterial infections to get started.

A mosquito bites its victim.

Insects and arachnids account for almost all the bites North Americans suffer, but they are identified less easily than any others. If a dog, a rodent, a horse, or even a snake bites you, you know that it has happened and which creature did it. If an insect or spider bites you, you may not even feel the contact of its mouth parts with your skin. You may realize you've been bitten only after an itchy bump develops a few hours later. Even if you did feel a bite, you probably could not identify the biter. Bugs are small. They move quickly. They have evolved superb methods of staying hidden. Only a small minority of biting pests are even seen, much less swatted or captured. More often, the victim is left to wonder what bit him.

It is often difficult even to tell whether the biter was an insect, a spider, or some other small creature. For example, consider the case of the brown recluse spider (*Loxosceles recluse*) and the deer tick (*Ixodes dammini*). The brown recluse is one of the few spiders in the United States able to inject enough powerful venom to cause serious medical problems for a healthy adult. The deer tick can carry the bacterium responsible for Lyme disease.

Especially in parts of the American Midwest, the recluse and the deer tick occupy the same territory. Either one could be responsible for a mysterious bite. Neither creature is often caught in the act of biting. Many people bitten by the brown recluse do not feel a thing until at least four hours later, by which time the spider is long gone. It takes several days before most deer tick bites are discovered. Each bite can produce the same external sign—a skin rash that looks like a bull's-eye target, with alternating rings of dark and light skin. With only the rash as evidence, a doctor has to guess which treatment is appropriate.

A wrong diagnosis can prevent patients from getting the treatment they need. Lyme disease can be serious if not treated early by a simple course of antibiotics. Left untreated, Lyme disease causes heart disease or nerve damage in about 10 percent of those infected. If a doctor mistakenly diagnoses a tick bite as a recluse bite, the patient will not get the antibiotics in time. Similarly, if a doctor mistakenly diagnoses a brown recluse bite as a tick bite, the spider's venom will do greater damage. There is no real effective antivenin to neutralize the toxin (poison), but hormone therapy soon after the bite can prevent a serious condition called necrosis. In necrosis, tissues that come in contact with the toxin die. This can create deep pits in the skin and muscle and can kill all nerve cells where the toxin goes.

The frustrated victim of unknown bugs in her Manhattan apartment did not suffer from either Lyme disease or necrosis. Few people do. That does not mean she had things easy. We can easily understand as itching overtakes us after a day at the beach (sand fleas? spiders?), an hour on the bus (mites? flies?), or a few minutes of strolling through a grassy field (nearly anything).

READING COMPREHENSION

Mark each sentence as *T* (true) or *F* (false) according to the information in Reading 2. Use the dictionary to help you understand new words.

.... 1. The bugs that bit the Manhattan woman lived in her mattress.

.... 2. The fear of being bitten can create emotional problems.

.... 3. Scratching a bite can create health problems.

.... 4. Insects and spiders are the only animals likely to bite humans.

.... 5. Insects and spiders often go away long before a bite victim even discovers the bite.

.... 6. The consequences of failure to identify the source of a bite are mostly emotional, not medical.

.... 7. Lyme disease is spread to humans through contact with mosquitoes.

.... 8. If a doctor misdiagnoses a tick bite as a spider bite, the bite victim may be poisoned by unnecessary medication.

.... 9. Necrosis can be prevented by a simple course of antibiotics.

.... 10. The venom of a brown recluse can be neutralized by a chemical called an "antivenin."

READING STRATEGY

Use the information in Reading 2 as a starting point for a flow chart. In your notebook, describe one of these things:

- what happens following a bite by a brown recluse spider
- what happens following the bite of a deer tick carrying Lyme disease

To expand your chart, do some outside research on the process you choose.

STEP I VOCABULARY ACTIVITIES: Word Level

A. Many academic words are also considered formal words. Which of the target words in this unit (see the chart on page 127) are more formal synonyms for these informal words? Be sure to use the right forms of the target words.

Informal	Formal
1. attach	....
2. enough	....
3. guess	....
4. outside	....
5. start	....

B. Complete the sentences about Bee Sting Therapy (BST) using the target vocabulary in the box. Use each item one time. The synonyms in parentheses can help you.

chemicals	initiates	percentage
circumstantial	minimal	regime
in contact with	neutral	sufficient

.... **a.** Apitherapy uses .... produced by bees—including venom—
(*substances*)
to promote human health.

.... **b.** BST's advocates say it is .... to reduce the effects of a serious
(*powerful enough*)
inflammatory disease called multiple sclerosis (MS).

.... **c.** Scientists struggle to remain .... on the subject of apitherapy.
(*not taking any position*)
On the surface, it just seems like a weird idea.

.... **d.** It seems to have gained popularity through .... evidence,
(*situational*)
such as that only a small .... of beekeepers develop cancer.
(*proportion*)
That is not enough for most health professionals.

.... **e.** Many eventually have only .... control of some muscles.
(*very little*)
They may also experience problems with vision, internal organ function, or
brain function.

.... **f.** Perhaps the most controversial form of apitherapy is Bee Sting Therapy (BST).
The name says it all. Patients deliberately place bees .... their
(*against*)
skin and wait for the sting.

.... **g.** Proponents of BST claim that a steady .... of treatments
(*regular system*)
provides relief for sufferers of arthritis and other conditions involving
inflammation. Exactly how it does so has not been explained.

.... **h.** The inflammation in MS typically .... a slow deterioration of
(*starts*)
the central nervous system as it damages nerve cells.

C. Put the sentences in activity B into a logical order to describe BST. (More than one order may be possible.) Read your sequence to a partner.

The word *circumstance* comes from Latin words meaning "around" and "stand." In English, *circumstance* does not mean "standing around," but there is a connection to this idea. Circumstances are the general conditions surrounding a person, thing, event, etc.

D. Read the sample sentences that feature forms of the word *circumstance*. Then, answer the questions below in your notebook, using a dictionary as suggested. Compare answers with a partner.

a. The ice storm was an unfortunate *circumstance*, wrecking our plans to have a nice dinner out.
b. Under other *circumstances* I would say "yes," but I have too much work to do.
c. His presence at the store on the night of the robbery is just *circumstantial* evidence.
d. Bob disappeared under suspicious *circumstances*.

1. Put a check (✓) next to the word closest in meaning to *circumstances*. Consult your dictionary before you answer.

   .... periods .... intricacies .... commotions .... conditions

2. In each of these sentences, the circumstances "stand around" something. What is it?

3. Look at the sample sentences in your dictionary for *circumstance* and its forms. In those sentences, what do the circumstances "stand around"?

4. Does *circumstance* have any forms that are not used in the sample sentences in the box above? If so, what are they? Consult your dictionary.

STEP II VOCABULARY ACTIVITIES: Sentence Level

Pesticides are chemicals used to kill insects or other small organisms that cause problems for people. Some pesticides are relatively harmless to humans. Others have been shown to cause great harm.

E. In each of the situations below, a pesticide is used. For each situation, answer these questions in your notebook:

   a. What chemical is it?
   b. How is it being used?
   c. Do the benefits of the pesticide outweigh its risks? Why or why not?
   d. Under what circumstances should it and should it not be used?

Refer to the readings in this unit and your personal opinions.

1. Collars for cats and dogs often contain pesticides meant to kill fleas and ticks. Some collars contain a class of chemicals called *organophosphates*. In some studies, these chemicals show a connection to brain cancer, paralysis, and nerve damage in humans.

2. DDT is a pesticide that kills mosquitoes and other insects. In the past, DDT was blamed for almost wiping out many species of birds, killing helpful bees on farms, and causing premature births. Its supporters say its ability to kill mosquitoes helps reduce the spread of diseases like malaria. Malaria kills about 1 million people each year and makes about 300 million sick. No human is known to have died from exposure to DDT.

3. About 1 in 1,000 people infected with the mosquito-borne West Nile Virus die from it. In 2005, 119 deaths from the illness were reported in the U.S. DDT is the most effective and affordable pesticide available to kill the mosquitoes that carry it.

F. Discuss your opinions about the situations in activity E in a small group. Then, prepare an oral report that summarizes your discussion of one of the situations. Present your report to the class.

G. Look at these arguments for and against a worldwide ban on the use of DDT. Restate each idea in your notebook, using some form of the word in parentheses. Then, write a paragraph that expresses your own opinion. Try to use as many target words as possible in your work. Be prepared to read your paragraph or debate this issue in class.

For	Against
DDT does not poison just the places where it is used. By getting into the water supply, into fish populations, and other cross-border resources, it threatens the entire world. (*chemical*)	Before the U.S. banned DDT in the 1960s, it was sprayed over entire farms. Of course it spread through the environment. Now, DDT is used mostly as a spray for the walls of homes in mosquito-infested areas. (*minimal*)
Big chemical companies are no longer able to sell DDT in rich countries. They are eager to sell it instead to poor countries, regardless of the damage it might cause. Only a worldwide ban can protect relatively powerless citizens from this toxin. (*sufficient*)	Rich countries are able to keep developing nations poor and powerless by making sure malaria rates stay high. A ban on DDT would remove almost the only affordable tool these countries have for becoming healthier and more productive. (*circumstances*)
Widespread use of DDT has led to the emergence of resistant mosquitoes. In a sense, its use has made it ineffective. By stopping the spread of DDT use—and restricting it to true emergencies—we can protect the usefulness of this pesticide. (*neutral*)	DDT does not have to kill mosquitoes to provide protection from malaria. It is also a powerful repellant, effective even with mosquitoes resistant to it. It greatly reduces the chances that a human will be bitten by a mosquito indoors. (*contact*)

H. Self-Assessment Review: Go back to page 127 and reassess your knowledge of the target vocabulary. How has your understanding of the words changed? What words do you feel most comfortable with now?

WRITING AND DISCUSSION TOPICS

Malaria and Lyme disease are not the only vector-borne diseases causing problems for humans. There are thousands of others, perhaps hundreds of thousands. No one knows for sure. Nor does anyone know how many people suffer from vector-borne diseases. According to figures from the World Health Organization, at least 600 million people (most of them in the tropics) have serious vector-borne diseases. Those with less serious ones almost certainly bring the total to more than one billion.

1. a. Do a little research to find out more about one of these vector-borne diseases. How is it caused? Which parts of the world are hit worst by it? What kind of creature carries it? What are its effects on human health?

- yellow fever
- leishmaniasis
- trypanosomiasis
- dengue fever

b. Why are the tropics especially hard hit by vector-borne diseases?

2. Success at fighting or avoiding vector-borne diseases has made possible a lot of human achievements. For example, the Panama Canal could not have been built if yellow fever had not first been brought under control. Agriculture and livestock ranching have expanded into areas once uninhabitable because of vector-borne diseases. How were these victories over disease accomplished? Were those methods good or bad for the overall environment?

3. Reading 1 says that global warming might affect the spread of red fire ants. What other effects might climate change have on biting or stinging insects and arachnids? Why? How would the changes you mentioned affect human health?

Inside Reading 2

The Academic Word List
(words targeted in Level 2 are bold)

Word	Sublist	Location	Word	Sublist	Location	Word	Sublist	Location
abandon	8	L1, U7	attain	9	L1, U5	complex	2	L4, U2
abstract	6	L3, U5	attitude	4	L4, U6	component	3	L4, U3
academy	5	L3, U1	attribute	4	L3, U10	compound	5	L4, U6
access	4	L1, U2	**author**	6	**L2, U4**	**comprehensive**	7	**L2, U7**
accommodate	9	**L2, U7**	authority	1	L1, U6	comprise	7	L4, U9
accompany	8	L1, U2	automate	8	L3, U6	compute	2	L4, U8
accumulate	8	**L2, U4**	available	1	L3, U5	conceive	10	L4, U10
accurate	6	L4, U6	aware	5	L1, U5	concentrate	4	L3, U8
achieve	2	L4, U1				concept	1	L3, U1
acknowledge	6	L1, U7	behalf	9	L3, U9	conclude	2	L1, U6
acquire	2	L1, U4	benefit	1	L4, U2	concurrent	9	L4, U5
adapt	7	L4, U7	bias	8	L4, U8	conduct	2	L1, U9
adequate	4	**L2, U4**	bond	6	L4, U3	confer	4	L4, U4
adjacent	10	**L2, U3**	brief	6	L3, U6	confine	9	L1, U10
adjust	5	L4, U3	bulk	9	L4, U9	confirm	7	L4, U10
administrate	2	L1, U3				conflict	5	L1, U2
adult	7	L3, U6	capable	6	L1, U8	conform	8	L4, U7
advocate	7	L1, U10	capacity	5	L4, U9	consent	3	L4, U7
affect	2	**L2, U6**	category	2	L4, U5	**consequent**	2	**L2, U3**
aggregate	6	L1, U9	cease	9	L4, U10	considerable	3	L3, U8
aid	7	**L2, U7**	challenge	5	L3, U8	consist	1	L4, U2, U9
albeit	10	L1, U7	channel	7	L1, U3	constant	3	L4, U8
allocate	6	**L2, U6**	chapter	2	L3, U7	constitute	1	L1, U4
alter	5	L1, U1	chart	8	L3, U10	constrain	3	L1, U8
alternative	3	L1, U10	**chemical**	7	**L2, U10**	construct	2	L3, U1
ambiguous	8	L1, U4	**circumstance**	3	**L2, U10**	consult	5	L1, U6
amend	5	**L2, U9**	cite	6	L4, U10	**consume**	2	**L2, U2**
analogy	9	L1, U4	civil	4	L1, U4	**contact**	5	**L2, U10**
analyze	1	**L2, U3**	clarify	8	L4, U8	contemporary	8	L1, U7
annual	4	L1, U9	classic	7	L3, U9	context	1	L1, U4
anticipate	9	**L2, U3**	**clause**	5	**L2, U8**	contract	1	L3, U9
apparent	4	**L2, U9**	code	4	L4, U9	**contradict**	8	**L2, U2**
append	8	**L2, U10**	**coherent**	9	**L2, U5**	contrary	7	L1, U6
appreciate	8	L3, U5	coincide	9	L1, U5	contrast	4	L1, U7
approach	1	L3, U1	collapse	10	L4, U10	contribute	3	L1, U9
appropriate	2	L1, U8	colleague	10	L1, U5	**controversy**	9	**L2, U3**
approximate	4	L3, U4	commence	9	L3, U9	convene	3	L1, U4
arbitrary	8	**L2, U8**	comment	3	L3, U3	**converse**	9	**L2, U8**
area	1	L4, U1	commission	2	L3, U9	**convert**	7	**L2, U2**
aspect	2	L3, U4	**commit**	4	**L2, U6**	convince	10	L1, U3
assemble	10	L3, U10	commodity	8	L4, U6	cooperate	6	L1, U2
assess	1	L1, U8	communicate	4	L3, U2	**coordinate**	3	**L2, U6**
assign	6	**L2, U9**	**community**	2	**L2, U7**	**core**	3	**L2, U5**
assist	2	**L2, U5**	compatible	9	L1, U9	**corporate**	3	**L2, U2**
assume	1	**L2, U1**	compensate	3	L3, U4	correspond	3	L3, U9
assure	9	L3, U4	**compile**	10	**L2, U6**	couple	7	L3, U1
attach	6	L3, U7	complement	8	L1, U7	**create**	1	**L2, U1**

Word	Sublist	Location	Word	Sublist	Location	Word	Sublist	Location
crucial	8	L3, U10	energy	**5**	**L2, U5**	fundamental	5	L4, U4
culture	2	L4, U10	enforce	5	L4, U7	furthermore	6	L4, U9
currency	8	L3, U9	enhance	6	L3, U1			
cycle	4	L4, U5	enormous	10	L3, U8	**gender**	**6**	**L2, U8**
			ensure	**3**	**L2, U5**	generate	5	L1, U5
data	**1**	**L2, U3**	entity	5	L4, U5	generation	5	L1, U7
debate	**4**	**L2, U4**	**environment**	**1**	**L2, U1**	globe	7	L3, U2
decade	7	L1, U7	**equate**	**2**	**L2, U2**	goal	4	L3, U3
decline	5	L1, U2	**equip**	**7**	**L2, U3**	grade	7	L1, U7
deduce	3	L4, U7	equivalent	5	L3, U10	**grant**	**4**	**L2, U9**
define	1	L3, U2	erode	9	L1, U9	**guarantee**	**7**	**L2, U8**
definite	7	L3, U4	error	4	L1, U10	guideline	8	L3, U3
demonstrate	3	L1, U5	establish	1	L1, U6			
denote	8	L4, U6	estate	6	L4, U6	hence	4	L3, U5
deny	7	L4, U10	**estimate**	**1**	**L2, U10**	hierarchy	7	L3, U4
depress	**10**	**L2, U4**	**ethic**	**9**	**L2, U9**	highlight	8	L4, U3
derive	1	L4, U10	**ethnic**	**4**	**L2, U1**	hypothesis	4	L4, U7
design	2	L1, U1	evaluate	2	L1, U10			
despite	4	L3, U2	eventual	8	L4, U3	identical	7	L4, U5
detect	8	L1, U6	evident	1	L4, U2	identify	1	L4, U2
deviate	**8**	**L2, U8**	**evolve**	**5**	**L2, U7**	ideology	7	L4, U6
device	**9**	**L2, U3**	exceed	6	L4, U1	**ignorance**	**6**	**L2, U9**
devote	9	L3, U9	exclude	3	L4, U7	illustrate	3	L4, U9
differentiate	7	L1, U4	**exhibit**	**8**	**L2, U5**	image	5	L3, U5
dimension	4	L4, U5	expand	5	L1, U7	**immigrate**	**3**	**L2, U1**
diminish	9	L4, U4	expert	6	L3, U8	impact	2	L1, U9
discrete	**5**	**L2, U6**	explicit	6	L1, U3	implement	4	L1, U2
discriminate	6	L1, U10	exploit	8	L1, U5	implicate	4	L4, U7
displace	**8**	**L2, U7**	export	1	L1, U3	implicit	8	L1, U3
display	6	L3, U5	expose	5	L3, U5	imply	3	L4, U7
dispose	7	L4, U6	**external**	**5**	**L2, U10**	impose	4	L1, U10
distinct	2	L3, U7	extract	7	L3, U2	incentive	6	L1, U10
distort	9	L3, U6				incidence	6	L3, U10
distribute	1	L4, U8	facilitate	5	L4, U1	incline	10	L1, U7
diverse	**6**	**L2, U8**	factor	1	L3, U8	income	1	L1, U3
document	3	L4, U9	feature	2	L4, U1	incorporate	6	L4, U4
domain	**6**	**L2, U8**	**federal**	**6**	**L2, U3**	index	6	L1, U4
domestic	4	L1, U3	fee	6	L1, U1	**indicate**	**1**	**L2, U4**
dominate	3	L1, U5	file	7	L4, U6	individual	1	L1, U1
draft	5	L3, U6	final	2	L4, U3	induce	8	L3, U7
drama	8	L3, U5	**finance**	**1**	**L2, U2**	**inevitable**	**8**	**L2, U8**
duration	9	L4, U1	finite	7	L1, U9	infer	7	L1, U8
dynamic	7	L1, U5	flexible	6	L3, U9	infrastructure	8	L4, U6
			fluctuate	**8**	**L2, U7**	inherent	9	L1, U1
economy	1	L1, U7	focus	2	L3, U8	inhibit	6	L1, U5
edit	6	L4, U8	format	9	L4, U8	initial	3	L3, U7
element	2	L4, U1	formula	1	L4, U8	**initiate**	**6**	**L2, U10**
eliminate	**7**	**L2, U9**	forthcoming	10	L4, U3	injure	2	L1, U1
emerge	**4**	**L2, U1**	found	9	L4, U8	innovate	7	L1, U3
emphasis	**3**	**L2, U9**	foundation	7	L4, U4	input	6	L3, U6
empirical	7	L3, U4	framework	3	L1, U1	**insert**	**7**	**L2, U9**
enable	5	L3, U10	function	1	L3, U1	insight	9	L3, U7
encounter	10	L3, U5	fund	3	L3, U3	inspect	8	L3, U3

Word	Sublist	Location
instance	3	L1, U6
institute	**2**	**L2, U8**
instruct	6	L4, U2
integral	9	L1, U4
integrate	**4**	**L2, U7**
integrity	10	L3, U7
intelligence	6	L3, U8
intense	8	L1, U2
interact	3	L1, U8
intermediate	**9**	**L2, U7**
internal	4	L3, U7
interpret	1	L3, U3
interval	**6**	**L2, U5**
intervene	**7**	**L2, U8**
intrinsic	10	L4, U4
invest	**2**	**L2, U4**
investigate	4	L4, U8
invoke	10	L1, U3
involve	**1**	**L2, U3**
isolate	7	L3, U4
issue	1	L4, U2
item	2	L3, U10
job	4	L1, U1
journal	**2**	**L2, U6**
justify	**3**	**L2, U3**
label	**4**	**L2, U2**
labor	1	L1, U2
layer	3	L3, U4
lecture	6	L4, U2
legal	**1**	**L2, U3**
legislate	1	L3, U3
levy	**10**	**L2, U9**
liberal	**5**	**L2, U1**
license	5	L3, U9
likewise	10	L4, U5
link	3	L1, U8
locate	**3**	**L2, U1**
logic	5	L1, U6
maintain	2	L4, U1
major	1	L3, U2
manipulate	8	L4, U4
manual	9	L3, U10
margin	5	L4, U3
mature	9	L1, U8
maximize	**3**	**L2, U8**
mechanism	4	L3, U9
media	7	L1, U5
mediate	9	L4, U2
medical	5	L1, U2
medium	**9**	**L2, U2**

Word	Sublist	Location
mental	**5**	**L2, U6**
method	1	L4, U9
migrate	6	L3, U2
military	9	L1, U4
minimal	**9**	**L2, U10**
minimize	8	L1, U1
minimum	6	L4, U5
ministry	6	L1, U2
minor	3	L3, U7
mode	7	L4, U7
modify	**5**	**L2, U3**
monitor	**5**	**L2, U3**
motive	6	L1, U6
mutual	9	L3, U3
negate	3	L4, U2
network	5	L3, U2
neutral	**6**	**L2, U10**
nevertheless	6	L4, U10
nonetheless	10	L4, U7
norm	9	L4, U6
normal	2	L3, U8; L4, U2
notion	5	L4, U9
notwithstanding	**10**	**L2, U1**
nuclear	**8**	**L2, U7**
objective	5	L1, U10
obtain	2	L3, U6
obvious	4	L3, U7
occupy	4	L1, U9
occur	1	L1, U2
odd	10	L1, U8
offset	8	L4, U8
ongoing	10	L3, U3
option	4	L4, U7
orient	**5**	**L2, U5**
outcome	3	L3, U4
output	4	L1, U7
overall	**4**	**L2, U6**
overlap	9	L1, U7
overseas	6	L1, U1
panel	10	L1, U6
paradigm	**7**	**L2, U6**
paragraph	8	L3, U6
parallel	4	L3, U9
parameter	4	L4, U5
participate	2	L1, U8
partner	3	L3, U1
passive	**9**	**L2, U8**
perceive	**2**	**L2, U9**
percent	**1**	**L2, U10**

Word	Sublist	Location
period	1	L2, U6
persist	**10**	**L2, U4**
perspective	5	L3, U2
phase	4	L1, U8
phenomenon	**7**	**L2, U5**
philosophy	3	L4, U5
physical	3	L4, U4
plus	8	L4, U5
policy	1	L3, U3
portion	9	L3, U9
pose	10	L3, U1
positive	2	L1, U5
potential	2	L4, U8
practitioner	8	L1, U2
precede	**6**	**L2, U4**
precise	5	L3, U10
predict	**4**	**L2, U1**
predominant	8	L1, U8
preliminary	9	L4, U1
presume	**6**	**L2, U2**
previous	**2**	**L2, U5**
primary	2	L1, U1
prime	5	L4, U4
principal	4	L4, U5
principle	1	L3, U9
prior	4	L3, U6
priority	7	L1, U2
proceed	1	L4, U9
process	1	L1, U9
professional	4	L1, U5
prohibit	7	L3, U10
project	4	L4, U4, U9
promote	**4**	**L2, U6**
proportion	3	L1, U10
prospect	**8**	**L2, U6**
protocol	**9**	**L2, U4**
psychology	5	L4, U2
publication	7	L3, U1
publish	3	L1, U3
purchase	**2**	**L2, U9**
pursue	5	L3, U8
qualitative	9	L3, U9
quote	7	L4, U10
radical	8	L3, U4
random	**8**	**L2, U7**
range	2	L3, U1
ratio	5	L1, U8
rational	6	L3, U3
react	**3**	**L2, U6**
recover	6	L3, U4
refine	9	L4, U4

Word	Sublist	Location	Word	Sublist	Location	Word	Sublist	Location
regime	4	**L2, U10**	source	1	L3, U2	trend	5	L4, U6
region	2	L3, U1	specific	1	L1, U6	trigger	9	L3, U7
register	3	**L2, U2**	specify	3	L4, U6	ultimate	7	L1, U9
regulate	2	L3, U6	sphere	9	L3, U7	undergo	10	L4, U1
reinforce	8	**L2, U5**	stable	5	L4, U5	underlie	6	L4, U6
reject	5	L1, U7	statistic	4	L4, U7	**undertake**	4	**L2, U3**
relax	9	L1, U8	status	4	L3, U2	uniform	8	L3, U1
release	7	L4, U1	straightforward	10	L3, U4	unify	9	L4, U5
relevant	2	L4, U8	**strategy**	2	**L2, U5**	**unique**	7	**L2, U1**
reluctance	10	**L2, U4**	stress	4	L4, U4	utilize	6	L3, U8
rely	3	L3, U2	**structure**	1	**L2, U1**			
remove	3	L3, U2	style	5	L1, U4	valid	3	L4, U10
require	1	L4, U2	**submit**	7	**L2, U9**	vary	1	L3, U10
research	1	L4, U2	subordinate	9	L4, U3	vehicle	8	L4, U3
reside	2	L1, U2	subsequent	4	L1, U1	version	5	L3, U5
resolve	4	L3, U4	**subsidy**	6	**L2, U2**	via	8	L1, U4
resource	2	L3, U8	substitute	5	L1, U1	violate	9	L3, U6
respond	1	L4, U7	**successor**	7	**L2, U9**	**virtual**	8	**L2, U10**
restore	8	L3, U5	**sufficient**	3	**L2, U10**	visible	7	L3, U5
restrain	9	**L2, U7**	sum	4	L1, U10	vision	9	L4, U3
restrict	2	**L2, U9**	**summary**	4	**L2, U10**	visual	8	L3, U7
retain	4	L4, U3	supplement	9	L4, U10	**volume**	3	**L2, U4**
reveal	6	L3, U8	survey	2	L1, U3	voluntary	7	L1, U10
revenue	5	**L2, U2**	survive	7	L3, U2			
reverse	7	**L2, U7**	suspend	9	L1, U10	welfare	5	L4, U1
revise	8	L3, U6	**sustain**	5	**L2, U4**	whereas	5	L4, U2
revolution	9	L1, U1	**symbol**	5	**L2, U2**	whereby	10	L1, U4
rigid	9	**L2, U7**				widespread	8	L4, U10
role	1	L1, U5	tape	6	L1, U6			
route	9	**L2, U5**	target	5	L3, U10			
			task	3	L1, U8			
scenario	9	L3, U7	**team**	9	**L2, U6**			
schedule	8	L4, U9	technical	3	L1, U6			
scheme	3	L4, U3	**technique**	3	**L2, U1**			
scope	6	L4, U8	technology	3	L3, U8			
section	1	**L2, U5**	temporary	9	L1, U9			
sector	1	L1, U3	tense	8	L1, U10			
secure	2	L4, U6	terminate	8	L1, U9			
seek	2	L4, U3	**text**	2	**L2, U4**			
select	2	L3, U1	**theme**	8	**L2, U2**			
sequence	3	L3, U5	theory	1	L4, U4			
series	4	L3, U5	thereby	8	L4, U3			
sex	3	L1, U3	thesis	7	L4, U7			
shift	3	L4, U9	topic	7	L3, U3			
significant	1	L3, U10	trace	6	L1, U9			
similar	1	**L2, U1**	tradition	2	L3, U6			
simulate	7	L3, U1	transfer	2	L4, U1			
site	2	L1, U6	**transform**	6	**L2, U7**			
so-called	10	**L2, U8**	transit	5	L3, U5			
sole	7	L4, U1	transmit	7	L4, U4			
somewhat	7	L1, U4	transport	6	L4, U10